Study Guide and ****

for use with

Prepared by **RICHARD B. LEE**
UNIVERSITY OF TORONTO

and **REBECCA ROSENBERG**

NELSON / EDUCATION

Study Guide and Workbook for use with Cultural Anthropology, Third Canadian Edition

Prepared by Richard B. Lee and Rebecca Rosenberg

Associate Vice President, Editorial Director:
Evelyn Veitch

Editor-in-Chief:
Anne Williams

Acquisitions Editor:
Bram Sepers

Marketing Manager:
Heather Leach

Developmental Editor:
My Editor Inc.

Content Production Manager:
Karri Yano

Proofreader:
Janice Okada

Production Coordinator:
Ferial Suleman

Design Director:
Ken Phipps

Managing Designer:
Katherine Strain

Printer:
Thomson West

COPYRIGHT © 2009 by Nelson Education Ltd.

Printed and bound in Canada
1 2 3 4 11 10 09 08

For more information contact Nelson Education Ltd., 1120 Birchmount Road, Toronto, Ontario, M1K 5G4. Or you can visit our Internet site at http://www.nelson.com

ALL RIGHTS RESERVED. No part of this work covered by the copyright herein may be reproduced, transcribed, or used in any form or by any means—graphic, electronic, or mechanical, including photocopying, recording, taping, Web distribution, or information storage and retrieval systems—without the written permission of the publisher.

For permission to use material from this text or product, submit all requests online at www.cengage.com/permissions. Further questions about permissions can be emailed to permissionrequest@cengage.com

Every effort has been made to trace ownership of all copyrighted material and to secure permission from copyright holders. In the event of any question arising as to the use of any material, we will be pleased to make the necessary corrections in future printings.

ISBN 978-0-17-610500-6

CONTENTS

Introduction		iii
Chapter 1	The Nature of Anthropology	1
Chapter 2	The Nature of Culture	21
Chapter 3	The Beginnings of Human Culture	34
Chapter 4	Language and Communication	45
Chapter 5	Making a Living	59
Chapter 6	Economic Systems	71
Chapter 7	Sex and Marriage	84
Chapter 8	Family and Household	97
Chapter 9	Kinship and Descent	107
Chapter 10	Social Stratification and Groupings	118
Chapter 11	Political Organization and the Maintenance of Order	129
Chapter 12	Religion and the Supernatural	142
Chapter 13	The Arts	154
Chapter 14	The Anthropology of Health	165
Chapter 15	Cultural Change and the Future of Humanity	176

Study Guide and Workbook for use with Cultural Anthropology, Third Canadian Edition

INTRODUCTION: WHY SHOULD YOU USE THE *STUDY GUIDE?*

Your instructor may or may not require the use of this study guide to accompany William Haviland et al.'s textbook, *Cultural Anthropology,* Third Canadian Edition. However, there are some important reasons why you might find it helpful as you begin your study of anthropology.

First, using a study guide along with the main textbook for the course forces you to simply spend time with the material. You have probably found that when you think you have read an assignment for a course, often you actually can't recall much of what you read. By adding time to your reading for answering review questions, going over key vocabulary, and so on, you fix the information in your memory in a far more thorough manner. The time you spend each day on your study guide will help you to spend less time "cramming" for exams later on.

Second, putting things in your own words, as the study guide requires, is the best way to make the subject your own. Education researchers agree that this is a good way to ensure that simple memorization is replaced by true comprehension of information. In addition, the exercises which encourage you to grasp concepts rather than memorize words will help you on tests, where your instructor may phrase things in different ways than your textbook author does. Make the book your own; write in it; do the exercises you find useful and skip the ones you don't. This guide was prepared to help you.

Each chapter of the Study Guide and Workbook contains several sections. A *synopsis* of the chapter is followed by an outline of *chapter objectives.* Then there is a section of *key terms* for you to define or identify and a list of *review questions,* which can be answered in a few sentences. There is also a *fill-in-the-blank* section to help you review. In addition to *exercises,* which range from the very difficult to the playful, there are *multiple-choice practice questions, true/false practice questions, practice matching sets, short answer questions,* and *practice essays.* These are excellent ways of preparing for the various kinds of examinations your instructor may prepare. Your instructor may also choose to use parts of this study guide for homework or extra credit assignments. If used conscientiously this book will be a helpful complement to your textbook.

For the Canadian Edition of the Study Guide, we have ensured that all sample test questions correspond with the content of the Third Canadian Edition. This process involved framing over 250 questions that were formulated specifically for this edition and are unique to this study guide. The result is that this Study Guide touches on all high points of the text that were developed specifically for Canadian readers.

Richard B. Lee and Rebecca Rosenberg

Study Guide and Workbook for use with Cultural Anthropology, Third Canadian Edition

CHAPTER 1
THE NATURE OF ANTHROPOLOGY

SYNOPSIS

Challenge Issues: What is anthropology? What do anthropologists do and how do they do it? How does anthropology compare to other disciplines? This chapter introduces the discipline of anthropology as the study of humankind and challenges us to consider the astounding degree of adaptation that humanity has made over time and place. There are five major fields/subdisciplines of anthropology: biological anthropology, archaeology, linguistic anthropology, applied anthropology, and sociocultural anthropology. Each of these seeks to produce useful generalizations about people and their behaviour, to arrive at the fullest possible understanding of human diversity, and to understand those things that all human beings have in common. Using examples such as the cultural differences related to human organ transplant, infant sleeping patterns, traditional healers versus modern medical practitioners, and the excavation and analysis of recent skeletal remains to investigate human rights violations around the world, this chapter explores the relevance of anthropology in today's increasingly globalized world.

CHAPTER OBJECTIVES

- the development of anthropology
- the discipline of anthropology
- anthropology and science
- anthropology of gender
- anthropology and the humanities
- anthropology's contributions to other disciplines
- the question of ethics
- anthropology and contemporary life

KEY TERMS

androcentrism
anthropology
archaeology
biological anthropology
colonialism
cross-cultural comparison
cultural imperialism
descriptive linguistics
ethnography

ethnohistory
ethnology
feminist anthropology
forensic anthropology
gender
historic archaeology
historical linguistics
holistic perspective
key informants

linguistic anthropology
paleoanthropology
participant observation
popular culture
prehistoric archaeology
primatology
sociolinguistics

Chapter 1 ➤ The Nature of Anthropology

EXERCISES

Review Questions

1. What are the five subdisciplines (or fields) of anthropology? How are they related to each other?

2. In their research, how do anthropologists attempt to be as objective and free from cultural bias as possible?

3. Distinguish between ethnology and ethnography.

4. Explain in what sense anthropology is a relatively recent product of Western civilization.

5. How does anthropology use the research of many other disciplines?

6. What is a holistic perspective and why is it important to anthropology?

7. Cultural adaptation, development, and evolution are three general concerns of anthropologists. How are they interrelated?

8. Why do archaeologists excavate sites from a historical period when many documents provide information on recent culture?

9. What is the significance of "The Garbage Project?"

10. Who are Franz Boas and James A. Teit?

11. With what aspects of language are linguists concerned?

12. Distinguish between the social sciences and the humanities.

13. Discuss how human behaviour and biology are inextricably intertwined. Provide examples.

14. Explain why it took so long for a systematic discipline of anthropology to appear.

15. Explain how the work of an anthropological linguist can contribute to our understanding of the human past.

16. Discuss the problems inherent in the science of anthropology.

17. Discuss the ethical problems that could arise in the process of anthropological research.

18. Describe the role of the ethnologist, giving an example of the sort of study an ethnologist would produce.

19. What is participant-observation? What are its advantages and disadvantages when compared to other social science methods?

20. Why might it be advisable to do research outside one's own culture prior to studying one's own?

21. What is meant by cross-cultural comparison? What significance does it have?

22. What is researcher bias and how can it affect ethnographic fieldwork and research?

23. What is the importance of fieldwork in the subdisciplines of anthropology?

24. What is globalization and why is it increasingly important today?

25. What is the role of applied anthropology in addressing cross-cultural health issues around the world?

26. What is the difference between a hypothesis and a theory?

27. What might be accomplished by research into one particular culture?

28. What distinguishes anthropology from the "hard sciences?"

29. Why must anthropologists exercise caution prior to publishing the results of their research?

30. To whom are anthropologists ultimately responsible?

31. What is the role of imagination in the development of science?

32. What are the dangers of culture-bound theories?

Fill-in-the-Blank

1. Anthropology is the study of _____ everywhere, throughout time.
2. Over the last _____ years anthropology has emerged as a tradition of scientific inquiry.
3. Anthropologists recognize that human behaviour has both _____ and social/cultural aspects.
4. Anthropology is divided into five fields: _____, _____, _____, _____, and _____.
5. An example of a practical application of physical anthropology is _____ anthropology, in which anthropologists testify in legal situations concerning human skeletal remains.
6. Archaeology is the study of culture based on _____ remains.
7. An in-depth description of a specific culture is called a[n] _____.
8. James A. Teit's research challenged the _____ centredness of 19th and 20th century ethnographic research through his focus on the female experience.
9. A tentative explanation of the relation between certain phenomena (e.g., "The light failed to work because the filament was broken") is called a[n] _____.
10. The concept of *gender* was first introduced by _____ anthropologists.
11. Anthropology demonstrates that there is no _____ basis for the notion of human races.
12. The physical anthropologist applies all the techniques of modern _____ to achieve fuller understanding of human variation and the ways in which it relates to the different environments in which people lived.
13. _____ is the set of standards and behaviours attached to individuals, usually, but not always, based on biological sex.
14. The term _____ refers to worldwide interconnectedness, signified by global movements of natural resources, trade goods, human labour, finance capital, information, and infectious diseases.
15. The branch of anthropology that studies human language is called _____ anthropology.

Multiple-Choice Practice Questions

1. Anthropology is _____.
    a. the study of Western culture primarily through the analysis of its folklore
    b. the study of humankind everywhere, throughout time
    c. the study of nonhuman primates through behavioural analysis
    d. the study of the species Homo sapiens by analyzing its biological but not its cultural dimensions
    e. the analysis of humankind from the subjective perspective of one group

2. The systematic study of humans as biological organisms is known as _____ .
    a. linguistic anthropology
    b. cultural ecology
    c. cultural anthropology
    d. archaeology
    e. none of these

3. Anthropology differs from other disciplines that study humans in its use of _____.
    a. cross-cultural perspective
    b. evolutionary perspective
    c. holistic perspective
    d. comparative method
    e. all of these

4. Which of the following is not a field of anthropology?
    a. cultural anthropology
    b. genetics
    c. archaeology
    d. physical anthropology
    e. linguistics

5. As part of your job, you may study the frequency of blood types in human populations, watch the behaviour of monkeys and apes, or dig for early hominid bones from East Africa. You are a/an _____ .
    a. etymologist
    b. primatologist
    c. ethnologist
    d. physical anthropologist
    e. cultural anthropologist

6. Theories about the world and reality based on the assumptions and values of one's own culture are _____ .
    a. simplistic
    b. irrational
    c. culture-bound
    d. relativistic
    e. inductive

Chapter 1 ➤ *The Nature of Anthropology*

7. An archaeologist might attempt to_____.
   a. study material remains to reconstruct past cultures
   b. study present languages to reconstruct when they diverged from a parent stock
   c. study garbage to explain contemporary behaviour
   d. "study material remains to reconstruct past cultures," "study present languages to reconstruct when they diverged from a parent stock," and "study garbage to explain contemporary behaviour"
   e. "study material remains to reconstruct past cultures" and "study garbage to explain contemporary behaviour"

8. An archaeologist studies _____.
   a. potsherds
   b. paleoecology
   c. genetic drift
   d. garbage
   e. potsherds, paleoecology and garbage

9. _____ is that branch of anthropology concerned with humans as biological organisms.
   a. Archaeology
   b. Cultural anthropology
   c. Ethnology
   d. Physical anthropology
   e. Paleontology

10. The focus of anthropology is on both evolution and culture; as such it is able_____.
    a. to address the "nature versus nurture" question
    b. to address certain ethical issues
    c. to discuss the efficacy of various research methods
    d. to address the qualitative vs quantitative methods issue
    e. to address the political questions of the day

11. In-depth descriptive studies of specific cultures are called _____.
    a. ethnologies
    b. ethnobotanies
    c. biologies
    d. ethnographies
    e. anthropologies

12. The study of two or more cultures is called a/an_____.
    a. ethnology
    b. case study
    c. ethnography
    d. biography
    e. ethnohistory

13. Anthropologists doing fieldwork typically involve themselves in many different experiences. They try to investigate not just one aspect of culture (such as the political system) but how all aspects relate to each other (for example, how the political system fits with economic institutions, religious beliefs, etc.). This approach is called the _____ perspective.
    a. holistic
    b. ethnological
    c. sociocultural
    d. sociological
    e. culture-bound

14. Ethnographic fieldwork _____ .
    a. is usually associated with the study of wealthy elites
    b. is usually associated with the study of North American society
    c. is usually associated with the study of non-Western peoples
    d. can be applied, with useful results, to the study of North American peoples
    e. "is usually associated with the study of non-Western peoples" and "can be applied, with useful results, to the study of North American peoples"

15. In Canada, the term "pre-contact" is used instead of the term _____ .
    a. ancient
    b. extinct culture
    c. Inuit
    d. prehistoric
    e. primitive

16. Besides being interested in descriptions of particular cultures, the ethnologist is interested in

    _____ .
    a. teaching food foragers how to use time saving gadgets
    b. cross-cultural comparisons
    c. descriptions of nonhuman species
    d. promoting Western ways
    e. providing data to various government agencies to help them suppress certain groups

17. The goal of science is_____ .
    a. to discover the universal principles that govern the workings of the visible world
    b. to develop explanations of the world that are testable and correctable
    c. to eliminate the need to use the imagination
    d. "to discover the universal principles that govern the workings of the visible world," "to develop explanations of the world that are testable and correctable," and "to eliminate the need to use the imagination"
    e. "to discover the universal principles that govern the workings of the visible world" and "to develop explanations of the world that are testable and correctable"

18. Which of the following *cannot* be used as part of the definition of the term "gender"?
    a. social construct
    b. learned
    c. biological
    d. culturally defined
    e. none of the above

Chapter 1 ➤ *The Nature of Anthropology*

19. Which of the following was/were pioneers in visual anthropology?
    a. Clyde Snow, Franz Boas
    b. Clyde Snow, Suzanne Leclerc-Madlala
    c. Franz Boas, Matilda Coxe Stevenson
    d. Matilda Coxe Stevenson, Suzanne Leclerc-Madlala
    e. William Haviland, Franz Boas

20. On which of the following are theories in cultural anthropology usually based?
    a. intensive fieldwork done in a single society
    b. ethnographies from all over the world so that statements made about culture will be universally applicable
    c. worldwide questionnaire surveys
    d. intuitive thinking about society and culture based on experiences in one's own society
    e. the theories about culture formulated by the people one has studied

21. In the process of doing research, ethnographers involve themselves intensively in the lives of those they study, trying to experience culture from their informants' points of view. In this sense, anthropology is _____ .
    a. scientific
    b. humanistic
    c. radical
    d. conservative
    e. systematic

22. In the writing and dissemination of research material the anthropologist has to consider obligations to various entities. Which of the following would *not* be one of the groups the anthropologist would be obligated to?
    a. the profession of anthropology
    b. the people who funded the study
    c. the people studied
    d. the anthropologist's parents
    e. none of these

23. Linguistic anthropology is concerned with _____ .
    a. the description of language
    b. the history of language
    c. how language reflects a people's understanding of the world around them
    d. "the description of language" and "the history of language"
    e. "the description of language," "the history of language," and "how language reflects a people's understanding of the world around them"

24. Some anthropologists tend to avoid quantitative analysis because it can be_____
    a. reductive
    b. too time consuming
    c. dehumanizing
    d. "dehumanizing" and "reductive"
    e. too difficult

25. While researching among an unfamiliar culture, the ethnographer will enlist the aid of "key informants," who
    a. are members of the culture being studied
    b. help translate a possibly foreign language
    c. help interpret whatever activities are occurring
    d. develop a close relationship with the anthropologist
    e. all of the above

26. It was not until the late _____ century that a significant number of Europeans considered the behaviour of others different from them to be at all relevant to an understanding of themselves.
    a. nineteenth
    b. twentieth
    c. seventeenth
    d. fourteenth
    e. eighteenth

27. Cultural relativism is defined as:
    a. the concept that all cultures are somehow related
    b. the belief that all cultures are equally valid and must be studied on their own terms
    c. the need to compare one culture to another in order to understand it
    d. all of the above
    e. none of the above

28. One of the applications of biological anthropology is _____ .
    a. the study of corporate culture
    b. participant observation
    c. historical linguistics
    d. forensic anthropology
    e. linguistic anthropology

29. Although humans are all members of a single species, we differ from each other in some obvious and not so obvious ways. Which of the following would be ways that humans differ?
    a. skin colour
    b. the shape of various physical features
    c. biochemical factors
    d. susceptibility to certain diseases
    e. "skin colour," "the shape of various physical features," "biochemical factors," and "susceptibility to certain diseases"

30. According to your text, we may think of culture as the often unconscious standards by which groups of people operate. These standards are _____ .
    a. genetically transmitted
    b. biologically inherited
    c. learned
    d. absorbed by osmosis
    e. none of these

Chapter 1 ➤ *The Nature of Anthropology*

31. Which of the following is not a specialty of sociocultural anthropology?
   a. primatology
   b. ethnology
   c. ethnography
   d. ethnohistory
   e. participant observation

32. The archaeologist is able to find out about human behaviour in the past, far beyond the
   _____ mere years to which historians are limited by their dependence upon
   written records.
   a. 20,000
   b. 10,000
   c. 5,000
   d. 7,000
   e. 8,000

33. Anthropological research techniques are applicable for which of the following research subjects?
   a. the study of non-western peoples
   b. the study of health care delivery systems
   c. schools
   d. corporate bureaucracies
   e. "the study of non-western peoples," "the study of health care delivery systems," "schools,"
      and "corporate bureaucracies"

34. _____ is/are another hallmark of anthropology.
   a. Case studies
   b. Surveys
   c. Random sampling
   d. Cross-cultural comparisons
   e. None of these

35. Another name for the ethnographic method is _____.
   a. participant observation
   b. ethnography
   c. ethnology
   d. case studies
   e. none of these

36. One well-known Canadian forensic anthropologist is_____
   a. Sheila Brooks
   b. Bernardo Arriaza
   c. Jennifer Thompson
   d. Owen Beattie
   e. none of these

37. From skeletal remains, the forensic anthropologist cannot establish which of following?
   a. stature
   b. race
   c. sex
   d. marital status
   e. age

38. A pioneering linguistic anthropologist, who discovered the linguistic link between Siouan language and the Tutelos of Ontario is _____ .
   a. Margaret Mead
   b. Ruth Benedict
   c. Franz Boas
   d. Owen Beattie
   e. Horatio Hale

39. _____ worked among immigrant populations in the United States in order to combat racism.
   a. Franz Boas
   b. Bronislaw Malinowski
   c. John Wesley Powell
   d. Leslie White
   e. Fredric Ward Putnam

40. An explanation of natural phenomena supported by a reliable body of data is a[n] _____.
   a. hypothesis
   b. theory
   c. fact
   d. imagination
   e. symbol

41. Which of the following services is **not** one that forensic anthropologists are routinely called upon by the police and other authorities to do?
   a. identify potential archaeological sites
   b. identify the remains of murder victims
   c. identify missing persons
   d. identify people who have died in disasters
   e. identify victims of genocide

42. Among the skeletal remains studied by forensic anthropologist Owen Beattie are the remains of _____.
   a. Julius Caesar
   b. General George A. Custer
   c. victims of genocide in Bosnia
   d. climbers of Mount Everest
   e. members of the 1845-1848 Franklin Expedition

43. This female anthropologist proposed that gender is culturally defined, thus providing an explanation for the observed differences in the roles and expectations assigned to genders in various cultures.
    a. Matilda Coxe Stevenson
    b. Ruth Benedict
    c. Margaret Mead
    d. Laura Nader
    e. Martha Knack

44. The role of ethnographic fieldwork, if carried out properly, is:
    a. a coherent description of a culture
    b. to provide an explanatory framework for understanding the behaviour of the people who have been studied
    c. to allow anthropologists to frame broader hypotheses about human behaviour
    d. all of the above
    e. none of the above

45. Which of the following is a hallmark of anthropological research?
    a. library research
    b. writing books
    c. lecturing
    d. fieldwork
    e. administering questionnaires

46. Although the sciences and humanities are often thought of as mutually exclusive approaches, they do share some common methods for certain activities. Which of the following activities is not common to both the humanities and sciences?
    a. critical thinking
    b. mental creativity
    c. innovation
    d. data gathering
    e. none of these

47. The discovery in 1948 that Aborigines living in Australia's Arnhem Land put in an average workday of less than six hours, while living well above a level of bare sufficiency, called into question:
    a. the understanding that food-foraging people were lazy
    b. the notion that food-foraging people had little time for pleasurable activities
    c. the idea that food foraging is an easy and laid-back lifestyle
    d. that food-foraging people did not work hard for their subsistence
    e. none of the above

48. The genocides in Kosovo and Darfur would be of primary interest to which sub-discipline of anthropology?
    a. archaeology
    b. economic anthropology
    c. ethnology
    d. forensic anthropology
    e. linguistic anthropology

49. Feminist anthropologist _____ offered her insider's perspective on the practice of female circumcision.
    a. Margaret Mead
    b. Fuambai Ahmadu
    c. Matilda Coxe Stevenson
    d. Ida Susser
    e. Leslie White

50. _____ theories about the world and reality are based on assumptions and values of one's own culture.
    a. Culturally relative
    b. Physiological
    c. Culture-bound
    d. Applied
    e. Molecular

51. Anthropologists do their work within _____ subfields of the discipline.
    a. one
    b. two
    c. ten
    d. seven
    e. five

52. In anthropology, tentative explanations of observed phenomena concerning humankind are known as _____ .
    a. theories
    b. hypotheses
    c. opinions
    d. patterns
    e. facsimiles

53. As experts in the anatomy of human bones and tissues, _____ lend their knowledge about the body to applied areas such as gross anatomy laboratories and to criminal investigations.
    a. ethnographers
    b. linguistic anthropologists
    c. ethnologists
    d. biological and forensic anthropologists
    e. archaeologists

54. The study of living and fossil primates falls with the purview of _____ .
    a. primatology
    b. osteology
    c. paleopathology
    d. forensic anthropology
    e. archaeology

Chapter 1 ➤ *The Nature of Anthropology*

55. Which of the following areas would not be of interest to the biological anthropologist?
    a. genes and genetic relationships
    b. growth and development
    c. human evolution
    d. political behaviour
    e. human adaptation

56. If I were called by the local police department's crime scene investigation unit to identify a murder victim, I would probably be a _____ .
    a. medical anthropologist
    b. forensic anthropologist
    c. paleoanthropologist
    d. paleoarchaeologist
    e. forensic entymologist

57. Using anthropological knowledge and methods to solve practical problems falls within the realm of _____.
    a. ethnology
    b. ethnography
    c. medical anthropology
    d. forensic anthropology
    e. applied anthropology

58. Explanations for natural or cultural phenomena supported by a reliable body of data are known as _____ .
    a. notions
    b. inspirations
    c. theories
    d. hypotheses
    e. factoids

59. One may think of ethnology as the study of alternative ways of doing things. Moreover, by making systematic comparisons, ethnologists seek to arrive at scientific conclusions concerning _____ .
    a. healing traditions and practices
    b. the relationship between language and culture
    c. the function and operation of culture in all times and places
    d. human evolution
    e. enzymes, hormones, and other molecules

60. The Garbage Project was designed in order to study each of the following *except*:
    a. contemporary social issues
    b. religious and ethnic affiliations
    c. validity of survey techniques
    d. differences in people's perceptions of reality
    e. waste disposal challenges

61. The branch of archaeology tied to government policies for the protection of cultural resources is called:
   a. cultural resource management
   b. forensic anthropology
   c. molecular anthropology
   d. museology
   e. contract archaeology

True/False Practice Questions

1. Culture is preserved and transmitted by language and observation.
    True or False

2. While ethnography is the in-depth study of a single culture, ethnology is the comparative study of culture.
    True or False

3. Ethnographic fieldwork is never done in Western societies.
    True or False

4. Anthropology can best be defined as the cross-cultural study of social behaviour.
    True or False

5. Forensic anthropologists are particularly interested in the use of anthropological information for the purpose of debate, oratory, and rhetorical criticism.
    True or False

6. A forensic anthropologist can even tell from skeletal remains whether the deceased was right or left handed.
    True or False

7. What a forensic anthropologist cannot tell from skeletal remains are details of an individual's health and nutritional history.
    True or False

8. One of Teit's major contributions to early anthropology was his determination to present the voice and experience of women in the 1800s.
    True or False

9. All cases of forensic anthropologists involve the abuse of police powers, and evidence provided by them is often ancillary to bringing the guilty party to justice.
    True or False

10. Franz Boas is considered to be the "father of fieldwork."
    True or False

11. Since the subject matter of anthropology is vast, a single anthropologist is personally able to investigate everything that has to do with people.
    True or False

Chapter 1 ➤ *The Nature of Anthropology*

12. Anthropologists know that, if formulated correctly, their theories will be completely beyond challenge.
    True or False

13. Archaeologists are biological anthropologists.
    True or False

14. Ethnologists study languages throughout time to determine how they have changed.
    True or False

15. Anthropologists think of their findings as something apart from those of other social scientists.
    True or False

16. The subdisciplines of biological and sociocultural anthropology are closely related, since we cannot understand what people do unless we know what people are.
    True or False

17. Physical anthropologists just study fossil skulls; they would not be interested in studying the recently deceased.
    True or False

18. It has been demonstrated that anthropological research and sociological research always come to the same conclusion regarding the culture being studied.
    True or False

19. In a sense, one may think of ethnology as the study of alternative ways of doing things.
    True or False

20. Anthropologists tend to view the world from a singular, narrow perspective, rather than a holistic perspective.
    True or False

21. Cultural and physical/biological anthropologists share common interests in the interplay between human culture and biology.
    True or False

22. Because their differences are distributed independently, humans cannot be classified into races having any biological validity.
    True or False

23. In his account of fieldwork in the Kalahari, Richard B. Lee's gift of an ox to the Ju/'hoansi was greeted with thanks and gratitude, for it was massive in size.
    True or False

24. Anthropologists work within at least ten subfields of the discipline of anthropology.
    True or False

25. Though each of the five subdisciplines of anthropology has its own research strategies, they rely upon each other and are united by a common anthropological perspective on the human condition.
    True or False

26. The main aim of anthropologists is to develop reliable theories about the human species.
    True or False

27. Linguistic anthropology focuses primarily on the cultural aspects of language and, as such, has no connection with the discipline of biological anthropology.
    True or False

28. Biologically, humans are apes. That is, they are large bodied, broad shouldered primates with no tails.
    True or False

29. Anthropology is often described as a blend between the humanities and the law.
    True or False

30. Humans, because they differ from each other in many ways, can be categorized into several species.
    True or False

31. As long as a theory is widely accepted by the international community of scholars, it is beyond change.
    True or False

32. For anthropologists, a re-evaluation of their role as researchers throughout the fieldwork process is a necessary aspect of contemporary ethnography.
    True or False

33. Anthropologists are now paying much closer attention to living histories, through narratives and oral histories.
    True or False

34. Anthropological research can include searching through garbage.
    True or False

35. Gender is culturally defined.
    True or False

36. Anthropological research relies primarily on quantitative methods of study.
    True or False

Chapter 1 ➤ *The Nature of Anthropology*

Practice Matching

1. _____ Anthropology
2. _____ Biological anthropology
3. _____ Cultural anthropology
4. _____ Forensic anthropology
5. _____ Culture-bound
6. _____ Archaeology

a. Field of applied physical anthropology that specializes in the identification of human skeletal remains for legal purposes.
b. The systematic study of humans as biological organisms.
c. The study of humankind, in all times and places behaviour.
d. The branch of anthropology that focuses on human behaviour.
e. The study of material remains, usually from the past, to describe and explain human behaviour.
f. Theories about the world and reality, based on the assumptions and values of one's own culture.

Practice Essays

1. Illustrate the usefulness of ethnographic fieldwork in North American society by discussing research on infant sleeping patterns.

2. Discuss the characteristics of participant-observation and how this method contributes to ethnographic understanding. How is this method characteristically different from other methods of social science research?

3. Describe how anthropology is at the same time a social/behavioural science, a natural science, and one of the humanities.

4. Stephen Jay Gould said, "The greatest impediment to scientific innovation is usually a conceptual lock, not a factual lock." Explain what is meant by this.

5. Your textbook gives different examples to illustrate the relevance of anthropological knowledge in the contemporary world. Identify and describe those examples.

6. How does the work of medical anthropology serve the interests of public health?

7. What are some of the difficulties that arise when applying the scientific approach in anthropology?

8. How can a cultural practice affect human biology? Explain.

9. Who is Owen Beattie? Describe his work.

10. What is "ethnohistory" and how has it helped us understand cultural change? Use examples from the textbook.

11. Which of the five branches of anthropology do you find the most interesting? Explain.

12. Humans are the only species capable of studying themselves and the world around them. Explain why humans would want to study themselves.

13. What does Richard B. Lee's account of spending Christmas in the Kalahari tell us about the role of the anthropologist and the challenges of fieldwork?

14. What is the difference between scientific theories and hypotheses? Explain by using examples from your textbook.

15. What is feminist anthropology? What imbalance does it seek to address? Give some examples of feminist anthropologists from the text.

SOLUTIONS

Fill-in-the-Blank

1. humankind
2. 150
3. biological
4. biological, cultural, applied, linguistics, archaeology
5. forensic
6. material
7. ethnography
8. male
9. hypothesis
10. feminist
11. biological
12. biology
13. gender
14. globalization
15. linguistic

Chapter 1 ➤ *The Nature of Anthropology*

Multiple-Choice Practice Questions

1.	B	22.	D	43.	C
2.	E	23.	E	44.	D
3.	E	24.	D	45.	D
4.	B	25.	E	46.	D
5.	D	26.	E	47.	B
6.	C	27.	B	48.	D
7.	E	28.	D	49.	B
8.	E	29.	E	50.	C
9.	D	30.	C	51.	E
10.	A	31.	A	52.	B
11.	D	32.	C	53.	D
12.	A	33.	E	54.	A
13.	A	34.	D	55.	D
14.	E	35.	A	56.	B
15.	D	36.	D	57.	E
16.	B	37.	D	58.	C
17.	E	38.	E	59.	C
18.	C	39.	A	60.	B
19	C	40.	B	61.	A
20.	B	41.	A		
21.	B	42.	E		

True/False Practice Questions

1.	T	13.	F	25.	T
2.	T.	14.	F	26.	T
3.	F.	15.	F	27.	F
4.	F.	16.	T	28.	T
5.	F	17.	F	29.	F
6.	T	18.	F	30.	F
7.	F	19.	T	31.	F
8.	T	20.	T	32.	T
9.	F	21.	T	33.	T
10.	T	22.	T	34.	T
11.	F	23.	F	35.	T
12.	F	24.	F	36.	F

Practice Matching

1. C
2. B
3. D
4. A
5. F
6. E

CHAPTER 2
THE NATURE OF CULTURE

SYNOPSIS

Challenge Issues: What is culture? Why do cultures exist? Are some cultures better than others? This chapter presents the fundamental anthropological concept of culture. It is learned, shared, based on symbols, integrated as a well-structured system, and dynamic. Through culture and its many constructions, the human species has secured not only its survival but its expansion as well, using culture as a primary tool for individual and social adaptation. The chapter concludes by considering whether it is possible for anthropologists to evaluate and compare cultures.

CHAPTER OBJECTIVES

- the concept of culture
- characteristics of culture
- the importance of Trobriand women
- anthropology applied: anthropologists in policy development
- gender perspectives: gender inequities in the Canadian immigrant experience
- culture and change
- culture, society and the individual
- evaluation of culture

KEY TERMS

cultural imperialism	ethnic boundary markers	micro culture
cultural relativism	ethnicity	pluralistic society
culture	ethnocentrism	social structure
culture shock	human rights	society
enculturation	integration	subculture

EXERCISES

Review Questions

1. How is culture defined, according to your text?

2. Distinguish between "culture" and "society." Do they always go together?

3. Distinguish between sex and gender.

Chapter 2 ➤ The Nature of Culture

4. Give an example of a pluralistic society and consider what factors seem to allow the larger culture to tolerate subcultural variation.

5. How is culture transmitted?

6. What is meant by the "integration" of various aspects of culture? Give an example.

7. What is the role of enculturation in the transmission of culture?

8. How did Malinowski define the "needs" to be fulfilled by all cultures?

9. In what ways is the concept of popular culture linked to class?

10. What is the difference between an ethnic group and a subculture?

11. What changes have recently impacted many pastoralists in sub-Saharan Africa?

12. In what ways must a balance be struck between society and the individuals who comprise it?

13. How can the large-scale sacrifices of the Aztecs be explained?

14. Distinguish between ethnocentrism and cultural relativism.

15. According to Walter Goldschmidt, what aspects of society indicate how well the physical and psychological needs of its people are being met?

16. What was E. B. Tylor's original definition of culture in 1871? (This is a classic definition in anthropology, so you should be familiar with it.)

17. Approximately how old is human culture?

Fill-in-the-Blank

1. The culture concept was first developed in the _____ century.
2. Your text defines culture as "the shared ideals, _____ , and_____
    that people use to interpret experience and generate behaviour, and that are reflected by their
    behaviour".
3. When groups function within a society with their own distinctive standards of behaviour, we speak of
    _____variation.
4. Enculturation refers to the process through which culture is transmitted from one
    _____ to the next.
5. Cultural elaborations and meanings assigned to the biological differentiation between the sexes is
    called _____ .
6. Another name for a multi-ethnic society is a _____ society.
7. In Kapauku culture, gardens of _____ supply most of the food, but it is through
    breeding pigs that a man achieves political power.
8. There is a difference between what people say the rules are and actual behaviour; that is, the
    anthropologist must distinguish between the _____ and the real.
9. The most important symbolic aspect of culture is _____ .
10. Anthropologists and all reflective people must attempt to strike a balance between cultural
    relativism and _____ .
11. Pastoral nomadic people in Africa south of the _____ have survived droughts
    because of their mobility.
12. The members of all societies consider their own culture to be the best; thus all people can be said to
    be _____ .
13. Anthropology tries to promote cultural_____ , or the idea that a culture must be
    evaluated according to its own standards.

Multiple-Choice Practice Questions

1. The contemporary definition of culture has changed from the meaning given to it during the nineteenth
    century. Today, _____ .
    a. culture is seen as values and beliefs that lie behind behaviour, rather than as actual behaviour
    b. culture is seen as real rather than as ideal
    c. the term "culture" has been replaced by the term "society"
    d. culture is defined as objects rather than ideas
    e. the term "culture" is not used

2. One way to determine if people share the same culture is to observe whether they_____ .
    a. are dependent on each other for survival
    b. are able to interpret and predict each other's actions
    c. live in the same territory
    d. behave in an identical manner
    e. all of the above

Chapter 2 ➤ *The Nature of Culture*

3. Which of the following statements about society and culture is *incorrect*?
   a. Culture can exist without a society.
   b. A society can exist without culture.
   c. Ants and bees have societies but no culture.
   d. A culture is shared by the members of a society.
   e. Although members of a society may share a culture, their behaviour is not uniform.

4. Every culture teaches its members that there are differences between people based on sex, age, occupation, class, and ethnic group. People learn to predict the behaviour of people playing different roles from their own. This means that _____ .
   a. culture is shared even though everyone is not the same
   b. everyone plays the same role
   c. all cultures identify the same roles
   d. all cultures require that their participants play different roles, even though that means that no one can predict the behaviour of others
   e. every person plays the same role throughout his or her life

5. The cultural definitions of what it means to be male or female today _____ .
   a. are determined by biological differences
   b. are independent of biological differences
   c. stem from biological differences that today are relatively insignificant
   d. developed about 60 million years ago
   e. have no relationship to sex

6. When groups function within a society with their own distinctive standards of behaviour, we speak of _____ .
   a. subcultural variation
   b. social structure
   c. gender differences
   d. cultural materialism
   e. ethnocentrism

7. The Hutterites may be used as an example of a/an _____ .
   a. pluralistic society
   b. subculture
   c. integrated society
   d. world culture
   e. complex society

8. The process by which culture is transmitted from one generation to the next is _____ .
   a. enculturation
   b. pluralism
   c. adaptation
   d. cultural relativism
   e. subcultural variation

9. Which of the following statements is *incorrect*?
    a. All culture is learned.
    b. All learned behaviour is cultural.
    c. Culture is humankind's "social heredity."
    d. Culture is not biologically inherited.
    e. The process whereby culture is transmitted from one generation to the next is called enculturation.

10. The most important symbolic aspect of culture is _____ .
    a. art
    b. language
    c. religion
    d. money
    e. politics

11. Among the Kapauku Papuans of New Guinea, the fact that an attempt to eliminate warfare (which would create a balanced sex ratio) would affect the practice of polygyny, which would affect the economy (since women raise pigs and the more wives a man has, the more pigs he can keep), shows that culture is _____ .
    a. materialistic
    b. relative
    c. pluralistic
    d. integrated
    e. enculturated

12. Which of the following is not a characteristic of culture?
    a. shared
    b. learned
    c. based on symbols
    d. fixed
    e. integrated

13. Which of the following is the least restrictive society in terms of rules of sexual conduct?
    a. Kapauku
    b. Canela
    c. Amish
    d. Muslim Brotherhood
    e. Norwegians

14. Cultural relativism is an important counter to _____ .
    a. pluralistic viewpoint
    b. ethnology
    c. human rights
    d. integration
    e. ethnocentrism

Chapter 2 ➤ *The Nature of Culture*

15. In a recent qualitative study, it was determined that the main reason for stress in Pakistani immigrant families was _____ .
    a. loss of prosperity
    b. underemployment
    c. joblessness
    d. "underemployment" and "joblessness"
    e. homesickness

16. A culture must satisfy basic needs such as _____ .
    a. the distribution of necessary goods and services
    b. biological continuity through reproduction and enculturation of functioning adults
    c. maintenance of order within a society and between a society and outsiders
    d. motivation to survive
    e. all of the above

17. _____ refers to the position that because cultures are unique, each one should be evaluated according to its own standards and values.
    a. Ethnocentrism
    b. Cultural relativism
    c. Cultural materialism
    d. Adaptation
    e. Pluralism

18. Goldschmidt suggests that it is possible to decide which cultures are more successful than others by looking at which ones _____ .
    a. survive
    b. last the longest
    c. satisfy the physical and cultural needs of the people
    d. support the most people
    e. are the least emotional

19. A mountain people of western New Guinea studied in 1955 by the North American anthropologist Leo Pospisil.
    a. !Kung San
    b. Kaluli
    c. Basseri
    d. Kapauku
    e. Azande

20. We now know that any culture that is functioning adequately regards itself as the best, a view reflecting a phenomenon known as_____.
    a. cultural relativism
    b. egoism
    c. nationalist
    d. ethnocentrism
    e. individualism

21. The idea that one must suspend judgment on other peoples' practices in order to understand them in their own cultural terms is called _____.
   a. structuralism
   b. functionalism
   c. structural functionalism
   d. cultural relativism
   e. relative culturalism

22. Popular culture also symbolizes the struggle to maintain a distinctive social and/or cultural identity. Quilt making by the _____ is an age-old folk art that possesses cultural meaning.
   a. Doukhobors
   b. Ukrainians
   c. Ju/'hoansi
   d. Aztecs
   e. Kapauku

23. The Acadians of New Brunswick and Nova Scotia are descendants of approximately _____ French families who settled in Canada in the seventeenth century .
   a. 50
   b. 75
   c. 100
   d. 200
   e. 500

24. Canadian anthropologist _____ works as a senior policy analyst in the international affairs group at Heritage Canada. This is one example of applied anthropology.
   a. Julie Sunday
   b. George Simmel
   c. Dr. Lauraine Leblanc
   d. Leslie A. White
   e. Ruth Benedict

25. Cultural elements such as history, beliefs, traditions, language, dress, and food can be described as

   _____.
   a. religion
   b. ethnic boundary markers
   c. a belief system
   d. transformation
   e. pluralism

26. To insure survival of a group of people, a culture must do which of the following?
   a. satisfy the basic needs of those who live by its rules
   b. provide for its own continuity
   c. provide an orderly existence for members of a society
   d. have the capacity to change
   e. all of the above

27. Malinowski's fieldwork among the Trobrianders of Papua New Guinea failed to give adequate time and consideration to _____ .
   a. the role of men
   b. the role of women
   c. familial relations
   d. system of descent
   e. none of the above

28. In 1871, _____ defined culture as "that complex whole which includes knowledge, belief, art, law, morals, custom, and any other capabilities and habits acquired by man as a member of society."
   a. A. L. Kroeber
   b. Clyde Kluckhohn
   c. Edward Burnett Tylor
   d. Karl Marx
   e. Margaret Mead

29. Which of the following is *not* a characteristic of society?
   a. a group of people who share a common homeland
   b. a group of people who are dependent on each other for survival
   c. a group of people who share a culture
   d. a group of people who share a common identity
   e. All of the above are characteristic of a society.

30. To survive, a culture must_____.
   a. satisfy the basic needs of those who live by its rules
   b. provide for its own continuity
   c. furnish an orderly existence for the members of its society
   d. strike a balance between the self-interests of individuals and the needs of society as a whole
   e. all of the above

31. Gender differences are as old as human culture, or about _____ years.
   a. 5 million
   b. 2.5 million
   c. 100,000
   d. 250,000
   e. 1 million

32. The thesis that one must suspend judgment on other peoples' practices to understand them in their own cultural terms is called:
   a. ethnocentrism
   b. separatism
   c. social relativism
   d. socialism
   e. cultural relativism

33. The job of anthropologists is to abstract a set of rules from what they observe to explain the social behaviour of a people. To arrive at a realistic description of a culture free from personal and cultural biases, anthropologists must:
   a. make judgments on other peoples' practices to understand them
   b. examine a people's notion of the way their society ought to function
   c. determine how a people think they behave
   d. compare how people think they ought to behave with how they actually behave
   e. "examine a people's notion of the way their society ought to function," "determine how a people think they behave," and "compare how people think they ought to behave with how they actually behave"

34. Although citizens of the United States are fond of boasting that theirs is the finest health care system in the world, they are merely reflecting _____ of their own culture.
   a. nationalism
   b. cultural relativism
   c. ethnocentrism
   d. relativism
   e. euphemism

35. Through culture, the human species has secured not just its survival, but also its expansion. Which of the following would be examples of human expansion?
   a. settlements in the Arctic region
   b. flights to the moon
   c. settlements in the Sahara Desert
   d. the exploration of space
   e. all of the above

36. _____ was a pioneer in anthropological fieldwork techniques.
   a. George Esber
   b. George Peter Murdock
   c. Leslie White
   d. A. R. Radcliffe-Brown
   e. Bronislaw Malinowski

37. Among the Kapauku, descent reckoning through men, coupled with near-constant warfare, tends to promote_____.
   a. egalitarianism
   b. female dominance
   c. male dominance
   d. dictatorship
   e. cultural deviance

True/False Practice Questions

1. To say that culture is shared means that all members of a society behave in the same way.
   True or False

2. A pluralistic society always has subcultural variation, but not every society with subcultural variation is pluralistic.
   True or False

Chapter 2 ➤ *The Nature of Culture*

3. A larger culture is more likely to tolerate a subculture if their values and physical appearances are similar.
   True or False

4. Cattle herding is the mainstay around which all of Kapauku Papuan society revolves.
   True or False

5. A modern definition of culture emphasizes the values, beliefs, and rules that lie behind behaviour, rather than the actual observable behaviour itself.
   True or False

6. Cultures are dynamic systems.
   True or False

7. The Hutterites are an ethnic group in the Canada.
   True or False

8. There are some societies that have no regulation of sex whatsoever.
   True or False

9. There can be no culture without a society.
   True or False

10. Ants and bees instinctively cooperate in a manner that clearly indicates a degree of social organization; therefore they have culture.
    True or False

11. Though one's sex is culturally determined, one's sexual identity or gender is biologically constructed.
    True or False

12. Canada's immigration policy is deeply gendered.
    True or False

13. The most important symbolic aspect of culture is language.
    True or False

14. Learned behaviour is exhibited to one degree or another by most, if not all, mammals.
    True or False

15. If a society is to survive, it must succeed in balancing the self-interest of its members against the demands of the society as a whole.
    True or False

16. Global communication systems and mass media have facilitated the diffusion of popular culture from one culture to another.
    True or False

17. Cross-cultural studies show that homicide rates tend to rise after the death penalty is abolished.
    True or False

18. Deviance is the same in every culture.
    True or False

19. People maintain cultures to deal with problems or matters that concern them.
    True or False

20. A culture must have the capacity to change so it can adapt to altered perceptions of existing circumstances.
    True or False

21. Cultures are biologically inherited, rather than learned.
    True or False

22. Humans do everything because it is adaptive to a particular environment.
    True or False

23. What is adaptive in one context may be seriously maladaptive in another.
    True or False

24. In any culture, some differences exist between male and female roles.
    True or False

25. For a culture to function properly, its various parts must be consistent with each other because consistency means harmony.
    True or False

26. Anthropologists seldom look at the archaeological or historical record to test hypotheses about culture change.
    True or False

Practice Matching

Match the culture with its description.

1. _____   Acadians
2. _____   Trobrianders
3. _____   Kapauku Papuans
4. _____   Aztecs
5. _____   Hutterites

a. descendents of the French, now facing economic problems
b. a Pacific Island people studied by Malinowski
c. a pacifist agrarian subculture found in Canada
d. a New Guinea people who breed pigs
e. a civilization in Mexico that engaged in large-scale sacrifices

Short Answer

1. What must be done for a culture to function properly?

2. What is meant by the statement "culture is dynamic"?

3. What happens when a culture is too rigid?

4. Although people maintain cultures to deal with problems, it is clear that some cultural practices prove to be maladaptive and actually create new problems. Provide examples of cultural practices that have proved maladaptive, creating new problems.

5. In what ways is Canada's immigration policy gender biased?

6. Who was Marius Barbeau? Describe his contributions to early Canadian ethnography.

7. Are animals other than humans capable of culture?

8. Explain why people maintain cultures.

Practice Essays

1. Using the Hutterites as an example of subcultural variation, discuss some of the factors that seem to determine whether or not subcultural variation is tolerated by the larger culture.

2. Distinguish between the concepts of culture and society.

3. Discuss the distinction between sex and gender and explain why this distinction is important.

4. Discuss the interrelatedness of the various parts of Kapauku culture. Use examples.

5. How does culture balance the needs of the individual with the needs of society?

6. Provide examples to support the statement, "What is adaptive in one context may be seriously maladaptive in another."

7. Using the example of the Kapauku Papuans, explain the idea that culture is integrated.

8. Anthropologist James Peacock wrote a book called *The Anthropological Lens* in which he compared culture to a lens or glass through which people experience the world. The anthropologist, then, is like an oculist who hopes to find the "formula" of each kind of lens, acquiring a kind of stereoscopy, or depth perception, by being able to perceive things through multiple lenses. How is culture like a lens? What are the limitations of this metaphor for understanding culture and anthropology?

9. What is cultural relativism and how does it impact anthropology as a discipline?

10. Describe Annette B. Weiner's research among the Trobrianders of Papua New Guinea. Consider the ways in which her research challenged earlier work by famed anthropologist Bronislaw Malinowski.

SOLUTIONS

Fill-in-the-Blank

1. nineteenth
2. values, beliefs
3. subcultural
4. generation
5. gender
6. pluralistic
7. sweet potatoes
8. ideal
9. language
10. human rights
11. Sahara
12. ethnocentric
13. relativity

Multiple-Choice Practice Questions

1. A		**14.** E		**27.** B	
2. B		**15.** D		**28.** C	
3. A		**16.** E		**29.** E	
4. A		**17.** B		**30.** E	
5. C		**18.** C		**31.** B	
6. A		**19.** D		**32.** E	
7. B		**20.** D		**33.** E	
8. A		**21.** D		**34.** C	
9. B		**22.** A		**35.** E	
10. B		**23.** C		**36.** E	
11. D		**24.** A		**37.** C	
12. D		**25.** B			
13. B		**26.** E			

True/False Practice Questions

1. F		**10.** F		**19.** T	
2. T		**11.** F		**20.** T	
3. T		**12.** T		**21.** F	
4. F		**13.** T		**22.** F	
5. T		**14.** T		**23.** T	
6. T		**15.** T		**24.** T	
7. T		**16.** T		**25.** T	
8. F		**17.** F		**26.** F	
9. T		**18.** F			

Practice Matching

1. A		**3.** D		**5.** C
2. B		**4.** E		

Chapter 2 ➤ *The Nature of Culture*

CHAPTER 3
THE BEGINNINGS OF HUMAN CULTURE

SYNOPSIS

Challenge Issues: To what group if animals do humans belong? When and how did humans evolve? When and how did human culture evolve? Chapter 4 introduces the student to the anthropological study of the human evolutionary past through an examination of our closest primate relatives, the chimpanzees, as well as the biological, cultural, and ecological changes that occurred through the evolution from *Australopithecus* to modern *Homo sapiens*. This chapter also considers the possible gender bias in primatology.

CHAPTER OBJECTIVES

- humans and other primates
- human ancestors
- gender perspectives: gender bias in primatology
- anthropology applied: stone tools for modern surgeons

KEY TERMS

Acheulian tradition	*Homo georgicus*	Neanderthal
Australopithecus	*Homo habilis*	Oldowan tools
hominine	*Homo sapiens*	Paleolithic
Homo erectus	Mousterian	primate order
Homo ergaster	natural selection	Upper Paleolithic peoples

EXERCISES

Review Questions

1. Distinguish between the terms evolution, natural selection, and adaptation.

2. What is the importance of cultural adaptation?

3. When did human culture first emerge?

4. Describe some of the early classification schemes used for humans.

5. To which order do humans belong and what other types of mammals are also included in this order?

6. Describe the evolutionary changes that occurred in primate dentition, sight, and touch; and also in the primate brain and skeleton.

7. What was the adaptive advantage in binocular stereoscopic colour vision among primates?

8. Describe the social structure of chimpanzee communities.

9. Describe what specific aspects of orangutan life Biruté Galdikas researched, as well as her motivations behind studying the wild orangutans in Borneo.

10. What is the role of hunting within chimpanzee communities?

11. Describe sexual activity among chimpanzees.

12. Describe some of the factors and concerns surrounding gender bias in primatology. Give examples.

13. What are the hallmarks of being human?

14. Discuss the significance of bipedalism. What changes resulted from this change in locomotion?

15. What was the role of meat consumption in human evolution?

16. What is the Oldowan Tool Tradition?

17. What role did tool-making play in human evolution?

18. What migratory patterns were associated with the Genus *Homo?*

19. What evolutionary advantages were conferred on *H. erectus* through the control of fire?

20. Who were the *Homo florensiensis* and how was their physical environment reflected in their in body size?

Chapter 3 ➤ *The Beginnings of Human Culture*

21. What is the Mousterian tool tradition? With what group of hominoids is it associated?

22. Describe and discuss the debate surrounding the emergence of modern *Homo sapiens*.

Fill-in-the-Blank

1. _____ specialize in the behaviour and biology of living primates and their evolutionary history.
2. A _____ is an anthropologist that specializes in the study of human evolutionary history.
3. A complex set of ideas, activities, and technologies that enable people to survive and even thrive in their environment is_____.
4. Humans are classified as a _____ because they are members of a subgroup of mammals that also includes lemurs, tarsiers, monkeys, and apes.
5. A group of individuals able to interbreed and produce viable offspring is called a _____.
6. The ability to see the world in three dimensions is called _____ .
7. The earliest identifiable tools are referred to as _____ tools.
8. Upright walking on two feet is called _____.
9. The latter of the Stone Age was called the _____ .
10. Shortly after 2 million years ago the species _____ appeared.
11. The tool industry found among the Neanderthals was called _____ .

Multiple-Choice Practice Questions

1. Which of the following studies living primates?
   a. palaeontologists
   b. paleoanthropologists
   c. primatologists
   d. ethnologists
   e. apologists

2. Which of the following operates on the level of a population through genetic change?
   a. adjustment
   b. natural variation
   c. adaptation
   d. evolution
   e. natural selection

3. When do paleoanthropologists believe that human culture first emerged?
   a. 1.5 million years ago
   b. 2 million years ago
   c. 2.5 million years ago
   d. 3 million years ago
   e. 3.5 million years ago

4. What is the basic physical unit of heredity?
   a. genus
   b. species
   c. allele
   d. chromosome
   e. gene

5. Unlike most other primates (excluding human beings), this animal can make and use tools.
   a. spider monkey
   b. chimpanzee
   c. squirrel monkey
   d. lemur
   e. none of the above

6. What is binocular stereoscopic vision?
   a. the ability to see the world in three dimensions
   b. the ability to see the world in four dimensions
   c. the ability to perceive depth
   d. the ability to hunt animals with visual skill
   e. the ability to see in all types of environments

7. What is the function of the vertebrate skeleton?
   a. provide overall shape to the organism
   b. support soft tissue
   c. protect vital internal organs
   d. all of the above
   e. none of the above

8. _____, the ritual cleaning of another chimp's coat to remove parasites and other matter, is a common chimpanzee pastime.
   a. tidying
   b. combing
   c. pinching
   d. grooming
   e. none of the above

9. Chimpanzees are known to _____.
   a. mainly eat plant food and invertebrate animals
   b. occasionally hunt and kill small to medium-sized animals
   c. exhibit teamwork behaviour when hunting baboons
   d. all of the above
   e. none of the above

Chapter 3 ➤ *The Beginnings of Human Culture*

10. One of Canada's most famed primatologists, who was known as one of "Leaky's Angels" and worked with wild orangutans in Borneo:
    a. Diana Fossey
    b. Jane Goodall
    c. Shirley Strum
    d. Biruté Galdikas
    e. Linda Fedigan

11. Chimpanzees are the only animals to use _____ in their process of conflict resolution.
    a. genito-genital rubbing
    b. mediation
    c. food
    d. aggression
    e. male dominance

12. Which primate(s) group(s) are our closet living relatives?
    a. chimpanzees
    b. gorillas
    c. chimpanzees and orangutans
    d. gorillas and chimpanzees
    e. orangutans and gorillas

13. Which primatologist studied baboons for many years and concluded that fieldwork is not biased toward males, believing instead that being a female has had no significant impact on her work.
    a. Kinji Imanishi
    b. Jane Goodall
    c. Shirley Strum
    d. Naomi Quinn
    e. Diane Fossey

14. Why was stone toolmaking and meat eating so significant in terms of human evolution?
    a. secured high quality protein
    b. led to the development of larger brains
    c. allowed for more leisure time, leading to further exploration and manipulation of the surrounding environment
    d. all of the above
    e. none of the above

15. Evidence of deliberate burials among the Neanderthal seems to suggest
    a. adaptation
    b. complex ritual behaviour
    c. natural selection
    d. ethnocentrism
    e. popular culture

16. Roughly 700 000 years ago, *Homo* _____ learned how to use fire.
    a. *erectus*
    b. *georgicus*
    c. *ergaster*
    d. *sapiens*
    e. *habilis*

17. Between five and fifteen million years ago hominoids lived in all of the following areas *except*
    _____.
    a. Africa
    b. North America
    c. Central Asia
    d. Europe
    e. Southeast Asia

18. Teardrop-shaped hand axes characterize the _____ tradition of tool-making.
    a. Oldowan
    b. Mousterian
    c. Acheulian
    d. Dmanisi
    e. none of the above

19. The earliest australopithecine fossils date back _____.
    a. 4.2 million years
    b. 3.6 million years
    c. 6.7 million years
    d. 1.8 million years
    e. 7.9 million years

20. Bipedalism, as opposed to quadrupedalism, is associated with all of the following changes *except*
    _____.
    a. increased ability to stand and see predators better
    b. increased ability to carry food
    c. increased ability to use tools as weapons
    d. decreased exposure to direct sunlight
    e. increased ability to run

21. Some anthropologists suggest that by _____ years ago, the only peoples on earth exhibited a physical appearance very similar to our own.
    a. 10 000
    b. 20 000
    c. 30 000
    d. 50 000
    e. 100 000

22. The discovery of *Homo* _____ challenged the commonly-held belief that *Homo sapiens* was the only living genus 20 000 years ago.
    a. *erectus*
    b. *georgicus*
    c. *ergaster*
    d. *floresiensis*
    e. *habilis*

23. *Homo erectus* fossils have been found in all of the following locations *except*_____.
    a. India
    b. Canada
    c. China
    d. Java
    e. France

24. *H. erectus* first emerged around_____years ago.
    a. 4.4 million
    b. 2.7 million
    c. 200,000
    d. 1.8 million
    e. 430,000

25. The controlled use of fire allowed for all of the following *except* _____.
    a. increase in the amount of potential social interaction with each other
    b. diminished hunting capacity
    c. greater nutritional value of foods
    d. softening of food, allowing the back teeth to get smaller
    e. increased control over the environment

26. The discovery of bones and small tools at _____ in the Yukon indicates a human presence there between 15 000 and 12 000 years ago.
    a. the Yellowsnake Caverns
    b. Quebrada Jaguay
    c. Debert
    d. Mont Verde
    e. the Bluefish Caves

27. The Neanderthals are associated with the _____ tool-making tradition.
    a. Acheulian
    b. Oldowan
    c. Mousterian
    d. Paleocene
    e. Levallois

40   *Chapter 3* ➤ *The Beginnings of Human Culture*

28. The period of the _____ tradition occurred between 40 000 and 125 000 years ago.
    a. Mousterian
    b. Oldowan
    c. Acheulian
    d. Levallois
    e. Neolithic

29. By the end of the _____ age, big game hunters had begun dispersing through North and, later, South America.
    a. Oldowan
    b. Mousterian
    c. Lower Paleolithic
    d. Upper Paleolithic
    e. none of the above

30. Obsidian blades, used by the Upper Paleolithic peoples, are superior to modern steel and diamond in the following way(s):
    a. up to 1050 times sharper than surgical steel
    b. up to three times sharper than a diamond blade
    c. easier to cut with and do less damage
    d. all of the above
    e. none of the above

True/False Practice Questions

1. Evolution is the principle by which individuals who have the best characteristics survive to reproduce.
   True or False

2. Adaptation is the source of biological variation that gives organisms a reproductive edge.
   True or False

3. Human culture came into existence 2.5 million years ago.
   True or False

4. Recent surgical tools have been modeled on the toolmaking tradition of the Upper Paleolithic era.
   True or False

5. Only humans have binocular stereoscopic colour vision.
   True or False

6. In monkeys, apes, and humans the cerebral hemispheres of the brain completely cover the cerebellum.
   True or False

7. Bipedalism allows for faster land movement.
   True or False

8. Biruté Galdikas studied chimpanzee behaviour in Northern Africa
   True or False

9. Chimpanzees frequently display a remarkable dependence on learned cultural behaviour.
   True or False

10. Some anthropologists, such as Shirley Strum, believe that there is no gender bias within the field of primatology.
    True or False

11. Male adult chimpanzees rarely, if ever, share their food with female chimpanzees.
    True or False

12. The hallmark of being human is bipedalism.
    True or False

13. The Oldowan tool tradition consists of hand axes, polished projectile points, and scrapers.
    True or False

14. The Mousterian tool tradition was found between 40 000 and 125 000 years ago.
    True or False

15. The consumption of meat and the development of tools had an enormous impact on human development.
    True or False

Practice Matching

1. _____   *Neanderthal*
2. _____   *Homo floresiensis*
3. _____   *Australopithecus*
4. _____   *Homo habilis*
5. _____   *Homo erectus*

a. a recently discovered genus, which has challenged earlier theories of human development
b. toolmaking allowed this genus to eat meat
c. has a brain size within the modern range, with a "primitive" looking skull
d. appeared less than two million years ago
e. earliest fossils date back 4.2 million years

Short Answer

1. What is the distinction between natural selection and adaptation?

2. Who was Biruté Galdikas?

3. What is a species?

4. Describe the evolutionary changes that occurred in primate dentition.

5. What is binocular stereoscopic colour vision?

Chapter 3 ➤ *The Beginnings of Human Culture*

6. Describe the sexual behaviour of chimpanzees in relation to the female menstrual cycle.

7. Why do chimpanzees hunt?

8. How are Japanese primatologists viewed, in terms of gender bias?

9. What are the primary characteristics of *Australopithecus?*

10. What are the adaptive changes that occurred with bipedalism?

11. What evolutionary advantages occurred as a result of controlling fire?

12. Who are the Neanderthals and why is there a controversy about them?

Practice Essays

1. How does evolution work through adaptation?

2. Describe the early attempts at human classification.

3. Why are humans classified as a primate?

4. Describe the primary evolutionary trends and tendencies among the primates.

5. What is the role of hunting within the chimpanzee community?

6. What is the role of tool-making in human evolution?

7. What is the relationship between locomotive patterns and environmental adaptation?

8. How did meat-eating contribute to human evolution?

9. What were the migratory patterns of *Homo erectus?*

10. Discuss the Neanderthal controversy. What are the causes of this disagreement and why is it a significant debate in our understanding of human evolution?

11. Why are surgeons today using the same types of tools used in the Upper Paleolithic era, and why are these tools doomed for extinction once again?

12. What is the "Eve hypothesis" and why has it been criticized?

13. Is the invention of tool use related or connected to human culture? Why or why not? Explain.

Chapter 3 ➤ *The Beginnings of Human Culture*

SOLUTIONS

Fill-in-the-Blank

1. Primatologists
2. paleoanthropologist
3. cultural adaptation
4. primate
5. species
6. binocular stereoscopic vision
7. Oldowan
8. bipedalism
9. Upper Paleolithic
10. *Homo erectus*
11. Mousterian

Multiple-Choice Practice Questions

1. C	**11.** B	**21.** C
2. D	**12.** D	**22.** D
3. C	**13.** C	**23.** B
4. E	**14.** D	**24.** D
5. B	**15.** B	**25.** B
6. A	**16.** A	**26.** E
7. D	**17.** B	**27.** C
8. D	**18.** C	**28.** A
9. D	**19.** A	**29.** D
10. D	**20.** E	**30.** D

True/False Practice Questions

1. F	**6.** T	**11.** F
2. F	**7.** F	**12.** T
3. T	**8.** F	**13.** F
4. T	**9.** T	**14.** T
5. F	**10.** T	**15.** T

Practice Matching

1. C
2. A
3. E
4. B
5. D

CHAPTER 4
LANGUAGE AND COMMUNICATION

SYNOPSIS

Challenge Issues: What is language? How is language related to culture? How did language begin and how do languages change over time? This chapter introduces the field of anthropological linguistics, considering how existing languages are described and studied and what the history of language can tell us. The three main branches of linguistics—descriptive linguistics, historical linguistics, and ethnolinguistics—are each examined as different approaches to the study of language. This chapter also explores the deeper roots of human language, from the gesture-call system to the origins of a uniquely human language and, eventually, to a writing system of visible or tactile signs. Furthermore, this chapter explores the ways in which language functions within a culture with reference to gender and bilingualism.

CHAPTER OBJECTIVES

- the nature of language
- the gesture-call system
- linguistic change
- anthropology applied: visual anthropology and ethnographic film
- language in its cultural setting
- gender perspectives: gender in language
- the origins of language

KEY TERMS

bound-morpheme
code switching
conventional gestures
core vocabulary
creole
dialects
displacement
ethnolinguistics
form classes
frame substitution
free-morphemes
glottochronology

grammar
kinesics
language
language family
linguistic divergence
linguistic nationalism
linguistics
morphemes
paralanguage
phonemes
phonetics
pidgin

proxemics
Sapir-Whorf hypothesis
signal
sociolinguistics
symbols
syntax
touch
vocal characterizers
vocal qualifier
vocal segregates
vocalization

EXERCISES

Review Questions

1. Why is language so important to culture?

2. What is linguistic anthropology?

3. What have ape studies taught us about human language?

4. Distinguish between a morpheme and a phoneme and give an example of each.

5. Distinguish between grammar and syntax.

6. What is the function of substitution frames?

7. What is the purpose of a form class?

8. What method does descriptive linguistics use?

9. What is paralanguage? Provide examples.

10. What are some of the factors contributing to language loss?

11. What is the "gesture-call" system?

12. Describe the Sapir-Whorf Hypothesis.

13. What are social dialects?

14. What is code switching? Give an example that you have observed.

15. What does glottochronology seek to explain?

16. Describe the importance of language for group identity.

17. What does ethnolinguistics seek to explain?

18. What are pidgin and creole languages? How are they related?

19. Why is the phenomenon of displacement important to study?

20. Describe the ways in which language can be sexist.

21. Your text notes that wild speculation about the origins of language is no longer necessary. What advances have been made that make such speculation unnecessary?

22. What types of communication have primates been taught?

23. What are the communicative capabilities of monkeys and apes?

24. What is the difference between a signal and a symbol?

Fill-in-the-Blank

1. The central and most highly developed human system of communication is _____.
2. A symbol has an arbitrary meaning determined by cultural convention, while a _____ has a natural or self-evident meaning.
3. Of all the potential sounds that can be made by the human vocal system, no more than _____ are used by any particular language.
4. The roots of linguistics go back more than _____ years, to the works of ancient grammarians in India.
5. _____ is the systematic study of the production, transmission, and reception of speech sounds.
6. The smallest class of sound that makes a difference in meaning is called a _____.
7. The smallest significant unit of sound that carries a meaning is called a _____.
8. The entire formal structure of a language is called its _____ .
9. Pronouns, lower numerals, and names for body parts and natural objects form the _____ of languages.
10. _____ refers to the extra-linguistic noises that accompany language.
11. The _____ - _____ hypothesis suggests that language predisposes people to see the world in a certain way, and thus guides their thinking and behaviour.
12. The English language reflects a long-standing ideology of _____ dominance in Western societies.

Chapter 4 ➤ *Language and Communication*

13. _____ is usually referred to as "body language."
14. _____ linguistics studies relationships between earlier and later languages.
15. English belongs to the _____ language family.
16. Linguistic _____ refers to the attempt by nations to proclaim their independence and distinctive identity by celebrating their own language.
17. The study of the relationship between language and social factors is called _____.
18. The process by which a person changes from one level of language to another is called _____.

Multiple-Choice Practice Questions

1. A system of communication based on symbols is called a _____.
   a. signal
   b. substitution frame
   c. language
   d. form class
   e. vocalization

2. All languages are organized on the same basic plan in that _____.
   a. they are all based on signals
   b. they take no more than fifty sounds and put them together in meaningful ways according to rules that can be determined by linguists
   c. they take no more than three thousand sounds and organize them according to the rules of grammar
   d. they all evolved from a common Egyptian language
   e. they originated in Russia

3. The modern scientific study of all aspects of language is_____.
   a. kinesics
   b. phonology
   c. linguistics
   d. grammar
   e. glottochronology

4. The systematic study of the production, transmission, and reception of speech sounds is _____ .
   a. linguistics
   b. morphology
   c. frame substitution
   d. phonetics
   e. syntax

5. Paralanguage is to speech as _____ is to position of the body.
   a. kinesics
   b. ethnolinguistics
   c. form class
   d. phonetics
   e. displacement

6. Consider the English word "dog." Which of the following is a morpheme?
   a. "d"
   b. "dog"
   c. "o"
   d. "g"
   e. "d," "dog," "o," and "g"

7. Which of the following is not part of the same substation frame in English?
   a. house
   b. cat
   c. daisy
   d. think
   e. car

8. The French-Canadian attempts to purge their language of certain English terms, such as *le weekend*, is one aspect of this phenomenon:
   a. code switching
   b. vocal characterizers
   c. linguistic change
   d. linguistic divergence
   e. linguistic nationalism

9. Which of the following is *not* part of the Romance subgroup of language?
   a. Spanish
   b. Romanian
   c. German
   d. Italian
   e. French

10. Kinesics is a method for notating and analyzing _____ .
    a. screaming
    b. kissing
    c. any form of body "language."
    d. fighting
    e. food

Chapter 4 ➤ *Language and Communication*

11. Descriptive linguistics _____ .
    a.   attempts to explain the features of a particular language at one time in its history
    b.   looks at languages as separate systems without considering how they might be related to each other
    c.   attempts to construct a language's historical development
    d.   investigates relationships between earlier and later forms of the same language
    e.   "attempts to explain the features of a particular language at one time in its history" and "looks at languages as separate systems without considering how they might be related to each other"

12. A language family is a group of languages that _____ .
    a.   all have the same core vocabulary
    b.   are subordinate to a dominant language
    c.   all have the same syntax
    d.   use the same number of sounds
    e.   are descended from a single ancestral language

13. If the core vocabulary of two languages is compared by glottochronologists, it is thought possible to determine _____ .
    a.   if the two languages perceive reality in the same way
    b.   if the two languages use the same syntax
    c.   if they share the same allophones
    d.   if they have a similar technology
    e.   how long ago the languages separated from each other

14. Linguist Michael Krause estimates that only _____ of the world's 6800 languages are presently safe from extinction.
    a.   100
    b.   300
    c.   600
    d.   1000
    e.   2000

15. Which of the following is *not* an example of linguistic nationalism?
    a.   You are a Cantonese-speaking person in Canada and want your children to learn English so that they can assimilate more completely into the society around them.
    b.   A national committee in France declares that certain widely used terms will no longer be allowed to appear in public print because they are not French.
    c.   You live in Scotland and are so alarmed by the rapid decline in the number of people speaking Gaelic that you start a school in which all subjects are taught in Gaelic.
    d.   The southern part of India declares itself a separate country called Tamiland (the land of the people who speak Tamil) in defiance of India's declaration of Hindi as the national language; people say they will die in defence of their "mother tongue."
    e.   A country previously colonized by the British passes a law requiring everyone to speak the native tongue; English is banned because of its association with colonial domination.

16. The influence of a person's class status on what pronunciation he/she uses, a speaker's choice of more complicated vocabulary and grammar when he/she is speaking to a professional audience, and the influence of language on culture are all concerns of _____ .
    a. descriptive linguistics
    b. historical linguistics
    c. ethnolinguistics
    d. linguistic nationalism
    e. displacement

17. The ability to refer to objects and events removed in time and space is _____ .
    a. dialect
    b. syntax
    c. displacement
    d. social dialect
    e. none of the above

18. The term _____ is usually used to refer to varying forms of a language that reflect particular regions or social classes and that are similar enough to be mutually intelligible.
    a. dialect
    b. language subgroup
    c. language family
    d. linguistic nationalism
    e. linguistic relativity

19. Which renowned Canadian anthropologist once stated, "Language is the hallmark of our species. It is upon language that human culture itself depends"?
    a. Benjamin Lee Whorf
    b. Edward Sapir
    c. Regna Darnell
    d. Asen Balikci
    e. Anthony L. Vanek

20. The very names for this dialect reflect the diversity of views. Which of the following are *not* terms used to refer to the type of English spoken by many inner-city African Americans.
    a. Ebonics
    b. African American Vernacular (AAVE)
    c. Black English (BE)
    d. African American Dialect (AAD)
    e. they are all terms that refer to Ebonics

21. The process of changing from one dialect of a language to another is known as _____ :
    a. bilingualism
    b. creole
    c. kinesics
    d. dialect changing
    e. code switching

Chapter 4 ➤ Language and Communication

22. A specialty within linguistic anthropology that has become almost a separate field of inquiry is
_____.
   a. sociolinguistics
   b. historical linguistics
   c. ethnolinguistics
   d. descriptive linguistics
   e. kinesics

23. This anthropologist made use of ethnographic films to challenge the simplistic and naive ideas about the Inuit held by many North Americans.
   a. Regna Darnell
   b. Benjamin Lee Whorf
   c. Edward Sapir
   d. Margaret Mead
   e. Asen Balikci

24. Although we are genetically programmed to speak, what we speak is determined by our   .
   a. parents
   b. teachers
   c. linguists
   d. culture
   e. genetic make-up

25. The first step in studying any language, once a number of utterances have been collected, is to isolate the _____ .
   a. verbs
   b. nouns
   c. phonemes
   d. adjectives
   e. adverbs

26. One of the strengths of modern descriptive linguistics is the _____ of its methods.
   a. subjectivity
   b. clarity
   c. objectivity
   d. simplicity
   e. consistency

27. In North America, scratching one's scalp, biting one's lip, or knitting one's brow are ways of conveying doubt. They are also what linguists call _____.
   a. morphology
   b. phonology
   c. sociolinguistic
   d. kinesics
   e. sign language

28. This approach concentrates on the way languages function now, as if they were separate systems, consistent within themselves, without any reference to historical reasons for their development.
    a. descriptive linguistics
    b. glottochronology
    c. diachronic linguistics
    d. historical linguistics
    e. phonology

29. _____proposed that a language is not simply an encoding process for voicing our ideas and needs but, rather, is a shaping force, which, by providing habitual grooves of expression that predispose people to see the world in a certain way, guides their thinking and behaviour.
    a. Benjamin Lee Whorf
    b. Noam Chomsky
    c. Paul Bohannan
    d. Emile Durkheim
    e. Robbins Burling

30. This branch of linguistics involves unravelling a language by recording, describing, and analyzing all of its features.
    a. social
    b. descriptive
    c. historical
    d. biographical
    e. phonetical

31. Language is embedded in a gesture-call system, also known as_____ :
    a. paralanguage
    b. emotions
    c. kinesics
    d. facial expressions
    e. nonverbal communication

32. The rules of phrase and sentence making is referred to as the _____ of the language.
    a. syntax
    b. morpheme
    c. phoneme
    d. bound morpheme
    e. kinesics

33. Specialists in this branch of linguistics investigate relationships between earlier and later forms of the same language, older languages for developments in modern ones, and questions of relationships among older language.
    a. descriptive
    b. social
    c. historical
    d. phonetic
    e. proxemics

Chapter 4 ➤ Language and Communication   *53*

34. The study of the cultural use of space is known as _____.
    a. ethnolinguistics
    b. historical linguistics
    c. kinesics
    d. paralinguistics
    e. proxemics

35. Only about _____ percent of Aboriginal children in Canada are learning their heritage language.
    a. 9
    b. 14
    c. 37
    d. 51
    e. 65

True/False Practice Questions

1. Your text traces linguistics back to the ancient grammarians in China more than three thousand years ago.
   True or False

2. Glottochronology assumes that the rate at which a language's core vocabulary changes is variable and thus cannot be used to give an exact date for when two languages diverged.
   True or False

3. Human culture as we know it could have easily existed without language.
   True or False

4. Though men and women in North American culture typically utilize slightly different vocabularies, the body language they use does not differ much.
   True or False

5. The emphasis on the French language by Québécois separatists is an example of linguistic nationalism.
   True or False

6. "Ebonics" is a substandard or defective dialect of English.
   True or False

7. Chimpanzees have demonstrated the ability to learn English as well as American Sign Language.
   True or False

8. Detailed knowledge of a culture's language is essential to a full understanding of the culture.
   True or False

9. Human language is embedded in a gesture-call system inherited from our primate ancestors.
   True or False

10. The study of language sounds is called morphology.
    True or False

11. The English language contains little to no gender bias.
    True or False

12. Kinesics is the entire formal structure of a language consisting of all observations about the morphemes and syntax.
    True of False

13. The French Creole spoken in Haiti is a result of the colonial era.
    True or False

14. Europe is immune to language loss.
    True or False

15. Most of the 53 Aboriginal languages in Canada are in danger of extinction.
    True or False

16. Of the nearly 6800 languages in existence today, nearly half are spoken by fewer than 2500 people.
    True or False

17. The idea that distinctions encoded in one language are unique to that language is called linguistic relativity.
    True or False

18. No language uses more than about 100 sounds to communicate.
    True or False

19. Human language is always embedded within a gesture-call system of a type we share with monkeys and apes.
    True or False

20. Cross-cultural research has shown few similarities around the world for such basic facial expressions as smiling, laughing, crying, and variations of anger.
    True or False

21. Like French, English distinguishes between feminine and masculine nouns.
    True or False

22. The effort by French Canadians to remove certain English words from their vocabulary is an example of code switching.
    True or False

Chapter 4 ➤ *Language and Communication*

Practice Matching

Match the term to its definition.

1. _____ morpheme
2. _____ phonemes
3. _____ form classes
4. _____ kinesics
5. _____ glottochronolgy

a. a method of dating divergence within language families
b. the smallest classes of sound that make a difference in meaning
c. the smallest unit of sound that carries meaning
d. posture, facial expressions, and body motion
e. the parts of speech that work the same in any sentence

Practice Short Answer

1. Identify the branches of the science of linguistics.

2. What is a morpheme? Define and provide an example.

3. Describe the gesture-call system. What are its various aspects?

4. What is linguistic nationalism? Give examples.

5. What is the Sapir-Whorf hypothesis? What does it tell us about language and culture?

6. Provide an example of a language that uses gendered speech and explain why it is considered gendered speech.

Practice Essays

1. Would it be accurate to claim language as a distinguishing feature of H. sapiens? Why or why not?

2. What evidence exists for the uniqueness or non-uniqueness of human language?

3. How is language linked to gender? Use examples from the text and add some of your own.

4. Discuss the importance and relevance of visual anthropology and ethnographic films. Make use of your text for examples.

5. Of central importance to the development of human culture is language. How might language have started in the first place?

6. Discuss some of the specific issues surrounding bilingualism in Canada. In what ways have issues of language divided the country?

7. Gender language reveals how women and men relate to each other. Exactly what does it reveal about how women and men relate?

8. Perhaps the most powerful force for linguistic change is the domination of one society over another. Provide examples of linguistic change brought about by colonialism.

9. Discuss the ways in which Instant Messaging language may or may not be changing the ways in which users communicate formally. Also, consider how IM has, paradoxically, prevented communication between members of different groups (parents and youth).

SOLUTIONS

Fill-in-the-Blank

1. language
2. signal
3. 50
4. 2000
5. Phonetics
6. phoneme
7. morpheme
8. grammar
9. core vocabulary
10. Paralanguage
11. Sapir-Whorf
12. male
13. Kinesics
14. Historical
15. Indo-European
16. nationalism
17. sociolinguistics
18. code switching

Multiple-Choice Practice Questions

1. C	13. E	25. C
2. B	14. C	26. C
3. C	15. A	27. D
4. D	16. C	28. A
5. A	17. C	29. A
6. B	18. A	30. B
7. D	19. C	31. E
8. E	20. D	32. A
9. B	21. E	33. C
10. C	22. C	34. E
11. E	23. E	35. A
12. E	24. D	

Chapter 4 ➤ Language and Communication

True/False Practice Questions

1. F
2. F
3. T
4. F
5. T
6. F
7. F
8. F
9. T
10. T
11. F
12. F
13. T
14. F
15. T
16. T
17. T
18. F
19. T
20. F
21. F
22. T

Practice Matching

1. C
2. B
3. E
4. D
5. A

CHAPTER 5
MAKING A LIVING

SYNOPSIS

Challenge Issues: What is adaptation? How do humans adapt culturally? What sorts of cultural adaptations have humans achieved through the ages and how has human adaptation differed from that of other animals? In this chapter the text examines the impact that various modes of subsistence have on cultures. Cultural adaptation and evolution create a dynamic interaction between organism and environment. Food-foraging and food-producing societies are described in detail, including the variations in food production systems over time.

CHAPTER OBJECTIVES

- adaptation
- foraging way of life
- gender perspectives: gender autonomy in foraging groups
- food-producing way of life
- anthropology applied: agricultural development and the anthropologist
- mechanized agriculture

KEY TERMS

anthropogenesis   horticulture   patterns of subsistence
carrying capacity   intensive agriculture   swidden farming
density of social relations   mechanized agriculture
ecosystem   pastoralism

EXERCISES

Review Questions

1. What purpose does adaptation serve?

2. Describe the relationship the Tsembaga have with the environment.

3. Explain what is meant by adaptation.

4. Describe the ways in which the Ojibwa adapted to the arrival of the Europeans.

5. What type of subsistence strategy is practiced by the Ju/'hoansi of southern Africa's Kalahari Desert? Describe.

Chapter 5 ➤ Making A Living

6. Provide an example of how a culture can be stable while not necessarily static.

7. Discuss the findings of David Damas' research.

8. What is pastoralism?

9. About how many people currently live by food foraging?

10. What previously held misconceptions of food foragers have been refuted?

11. What are the main social characteristics of food foragers?

12. What are the size-limiting factors in a foraging group?

13. Who are the Bakhtiari? Describe their subsistence strategy.

14. What impact does biological sex have on the division of labour?

15. Describe the two major research areas of Bruce Trigger.

16. Why are food foragers generally egalitarian?

17. Can we make any generalizations about the status of women in foraging societies?

18. How is territory conceptualized in foraging societies?

19. Discuss the division of labour among the Blackfoot of the Canadian Northern Plains.

20. Distinguish between horticulturalists and agriculturalists.

21. Describe the process of swidden farming.

22. Define "adaptation" and "ecosystem" and illustrate the relevance of these concepts with the example of pig sacrifices among the Tsembaga.

23. Why has swidden farming come to be viewed negatively by many people today?

24. What types of major innovations accompanied the process of urbanization?

25. Describe the characteristics of the Aztec state.

Fill-in-the-Blank

1. _____ is the process by which organisms modify and adjust to their environment and thereby survive more effectively.
2. A system composed of both the natural environment and all the organisms living in it is called the _____.
3. Prior to the arrival of the Europeans, the members of the Blackfoot Confederacy depended on the _____ as their primary food source.
4. Foragers are, by definition, people who do not _____ or practice animal husbandry.
5. The number of people who can be supported by a certain technology is the _____ capacity of the environment.
6. The Bakhtiari are an example of a _____ society.
7. Hunting, fishing, and gathering wild foods is called _____ .
8. The _____ is the number and intensity of interactions among the members of a camp.
9. Status differences among food foragers does not negate the fact that most food foraging societies tend to be _____.
10. _____ is technologically more complex than horticulture.
11. Humans lived using food foraging until about _____ to 11,000 years ago, when domestication of animals and plants began.
12. With the intensification of _____ , some farming villages became urbanized.
13. The Bakhitiari are known to engage in very limited _____.
14. About ___ percent of the diet of most food foragers is gathered by women.
15. Increased food sharing appears to be related to a shift in food habits involving increased eating of _____ around two and a half million years ago.
16. Another name for slash-and-burn is _____ farming.

Multiple-Choice Practice Questions

1. Adaptation refers to the _____ .
   a. process by which organisms modify and adjust to their environment and thereby survive more effectively
   b. ability of one population to destroy another
   c. borrowing of cultural material from another society
   d. process by which living systems change from birth to death
   e. effect of child-rearing practices on basic personality structure

Chapter 5 ➤ *Making A Living*

2. The Bakhtiari engage primarily in what type of subsistence practice?
   a. swidden farming
   b. intensive agriculture
   c. foraging
   d. horticulture
   e. pastoralism

3. Swidden farming is also referred to as _____ .
   a. intensive agriculture
   b. horticulture
   c. slash-and-burn
   d. foraging
   e. mechanized agriculture

4. The material goods of foragers must be limited to the barest essentials. For example, the average weight of an individual's personal belongings among the Ju/'hoansi is just under _____ kilograms.
   a. 4
   b. 8
   c. 11
   d. 13
   e. 16

5. Although foragers own little property, an interesting exception occurred among the _____, when horses became incredibly valuable possessions.
   a. Mbuti
   b. Blackfoot
   c. Ju/'hoansi
   d. Bahktiari
   e. none of the above

6. A subsistence strategy that relies on domesticated herd animals and usually requires seasonal movement to pastures is known as _____ .
   a. horticulture
   b. gathering
   c. hunting
   d. pastoralism
   e. foraging

7. Humans are particularly influential on their environment, causing a range of changes through a process known as _____ .
   a. adaptation
   b. evolution
   c. anthropogenesis
   d. foraging
   e. none of the above

8. Some anthropologists refer to food foragers as "the original affluent society" because
_____ .
   a. they manage to accumulate a lot of wealth
   b. they occupy the most attractive environments with abundant food supply
   c. they live in marginal areas and are very poor
   d. they earn a good wage for all hours of work they put in each week
   e. they work only twelve to nineteen hours a week for a comfortable, healthy life

9. The groups referred to as food foragers must live where there are naturally available food sources; thus they _____ .
   a. remain in permanent settlements
   b. move about once every ten years
   c. move frequently
   d. adopt farming whenever they can
   e. prefer to live in cities

10. The number and intensity of interactions among the members of a residential unit is called
_____ .
   a. density of social relations
   b. social interactionism
   c. cultural ecology
   d. carrying capacity
   e. convergent evolution

11. Which of the following is *not* one of the three elements of human social organization that developed with hunting?
   a. sexual division of labour
   b. aggressive behaviour
   c. food sharing
   d. the camp site
   e. "sexual division of labour," "aggressive behaviour," "food sharing," and "the camp site"

12. In a food-foraging society, how do people store food for the future?
   a. They keep a surplus in stone cairns.
   b. They keep extra plants in large, circular yam houses.
   c. They hide meat in each individual family residence.
   d. They tend to not accumulate surplus food (except in the coldest climate).
   e. They keep dried food in a common storage shed.

13. To say that food-foraging societies are egalitarian means that _____ .
   a. there are no status differences
   b. the only status differences are age and sex
   c. everyone is equal except women
   d. men are usually subordinate to women
   e. children are the centre of community life

Chapter 5 ➤ *Making A Living*

14. Someone who uses irrigation, fertilizers, and the plough to produce food on large plots of land is known as a/an _____ .
    a. horticulturalist
    b. agriculturalist
    c. pastoralists
    d. hunter-gatherer
    e. industrialist

15. _____ are food producers who specialize in animal husbandry and who consider their way of life to be ideal and central to defining their identities.
    a. Food foragers
    b. Horticulturalists
    c. Agriculturalists
    d. Pastoralists
    e. Industrialists

16. Aztec society in the sixteenth century _____.
    a. was a stratified society based on achievement and education
    b. was an urbanized society in which kinship played no role in determining status
    c. was an industrial city-state
    d. was invincible to Cortes's attack
    e. none of these

17. In foraging societies, _____.
    a. women tend to gather food
    b. men hunt for meat
    c. the work of women is no less arduous than that of men
    d. "women tend to gather food" and "men hunt for meat"
    e. none of the above

18. Which of the following is the oldest form of subsistence?
    a. slash-and-burn
    b. food-producing
    c. horticulture
    d. food foraging
    e. agriculture

19. The Hopi of the North American southwest traditionally employed irrigation in their farming, while using simple hand tools. This is an example of:
    a. industrialized agriculture / intensive agriculture
    b. intensive agriculture / horticulture
    c. urbanization / industrialized agriculture
    d. swidden farming / pastoralism
    e. pastoralism / horticulture

20. A society's cultural beliefs, no matter how irrelevant they may seem to outsiders, are anything but irrelevant if one is to understand another society's _____ practices.
    a. marketing
    b. voting
    c. business
    d. trading
    e. subsistence

21. How food-foraging peoples regulate population size relates to which of the following things?
    a. how much body fat they accumulate
    b. the accumulation of material goods
    c. abortion practices
    d. how they care for their children
    e. "how much body fat they accumulate" and "how they care for their children"

22. Which of the following subsistence modes is based on the herding of animals?
    a. food-foraging
    b. pastoralism
    c. slash-and-burn cultivation
    d. hunting and gathering
    e. farming

23. The _____ process establishes a moving balance between the needs of a population and the potential of its environment.
    a. adaptation
    b. accommodation
    c. integration
    d. evolution
    e. adjustment

24. The long-term stability of many foraging communities suggests _____ .
    a. stagnation
    b. backwardness
    c. failure to progress
    d. success
    e. none of the above

25. Bruce Trigger, a Canadian anthropologist/archaeologist suggested that several factors formed the basis for political unity for the powerful confederacies of the Iroquoian peoples in the sixteenth to eighteenth centuries. Which of the following *is not* one the factors?
    a. slash-and-burn horticulture
    b. long-distance trade
    c. pastoralism
    d. raiding
    e. diplomacy

Chapter 5 ➤ *Making A Living*

26. The number of people the available resources can support at a given technological level is known as the _____ .
    a. density of social relations
    b. equilibrium point
    c. carrying capacity
    d. point of diminishing capacity
    e. balanced position

27. Food foragers like the _____ have a division of labour in which women gather and prepare "bush" food, but hunting is usually done by men.
    a. Mekranoti
    b. Crow
    c. Ju/'hoansi
    d. Bahktiari
    e. Tutsi

28. Although we tend to think of people as either pastoral nomads or horticulturalists, there are numerous examples of people like the _____, who rely on a mix of pastoralism and small-scale farming for subsistence.
    a. Ju/'hoansi
    b. Comanche
    c. Aztec
    d. Bakhtiari
    e. Papago

29. Aztec agricultural success provided for which of the following?
    a. a highly mobile population
    b. an increasingly large population
    c. the diversification of labour
    d. a more egalitarian society
    e. "an increasingly large population" and "the diversification of labour"

30. Intensive agriculture, a more complex activity than swidden farming, requires which of the following?
    a. irrigation
    b. fertilizers
    c. draft animals
    d. a high level of mobility
    e. "irrigation," "fertilizers," and "draft animals"

31. Currently, most farming in the Canadian prairies is an example of _____ .
    a. simple horticulture
    b. pastoralism
    c. urbanization
    d. intensive agriculture
    e. none of the above

32. Which foraging group was part of the Canadian Northern Plains culture area?
    a. Iroquois
    b. Cheyenne
    c. Ojibwa
    d. Blackfoot
    e. Hopi

33. The Ju/'hoansi spend about 20 hours a week working to maintain an above-average level of nutrition and sustenance, while the Western workweek tends to be about _____ hours long.
    a. 33
    b. 37
    c. 42
    d. 64
    e. 75

True/False Practice Questions

1. Periodic frosts have made Altiplano agriculture in South America very challenging.
   True or False

2. The Mbuti live in the Ituri rain forest in the Republic of the Congo.
   True or False

3. The Bakhtiari are pastoralist nomads who drive their herds throughout the Iran-Iraq border area.
   True or False

4. Today, industrialism is declining rapidly.
   True or False

5. The spread of malaria was historically linked to the development of slash-and-burn horticulture.
   True or False

6. In the world today, about 3 million people live by food foraging.
   True or False

7. People started shifting to food-producing ways of life about ten thousand years ago.
   True or False

8. The average work-week of the Ju/'hoansi is about fifty hours.
   True or False

9. An anthropologist would probably find it difficult to define what "progress" is.
   True or False

10. Notwithstanding the multiple changes that have occurred over the course of many thousands of years, the original division of labour has been eliminated from every culture.
    True or False

Chapter 5 ➤ _Making A Living_

11. Everybody benefits from changes, even if they are forced upon them.
    True or False

12. All innovations turn out to be positive in the long run, eventually improving conditions for every member of a society.
    True or False

13. Slash-and-burn agriculture, especially in the humid tropics, may be one of the best gardening techniques possible.
    True or False

14. The Bakhtiari occasionally practice horticulturalism.
    True or False

15. Domestication resulted in the complete eradication of foraging.
    True or False

16. The high fertility of Amazonian garden plots comes from the soil, not from the trees that are burned there.
    True or False

17. By refusing to share, the Ju/'hoansi achieve social levelling.
    True or False

18. The nature of women's work in foraging societies makes it difficult to care for children.
    True or False

19. The Tsembaga highlanders of New Guinea mostly support themselves with a hunting and gathering subsistence lifestyle.
    True or False

20. Food foraging would certainly not be found in a rich industrial nation such as Canada.
    True or False

Practice Matching

Match the culture with its characteristic.

1. _____   Tsembaga
2. _____   Bakhtiari
3. _____   Blackfoot
4. _____   Mbuti
5. _____   Montagnais

a. live in eastern Quebec and Labrador
b. West Asian pastoralists
c. horse people of the Northern Plains
d. pig sacrificers of New Guinea.
e. food foragers of the Ituri rain forest

Practice Short Answer Questions

1. Explain what type of farming was used in Southwest Asia and Mesoamerica.

2. Explain why anthropologists have referred to foragers as the "original affluent society."

3. What are the social characteristics of an agricultural society? How do they differ from foraging societies?

4. Why do anthropologists *not* use the term "progress"?

5. Distinguish between food-foraging societies and food-producing societies.

Practice Essays

1. How does Ju/'hoansi social organization relate to the subsistence pattern of hunting and collecting? How is Ju/'hoansi society likely to change as the foraging way of life erodes?

2. Many communities employ what has come to be known as swidden farming. Describe the benefits of this style of farming in the tropics. What would be the consequences of Canadian-style industrialized agriculture in the tropics?

3. Many foraging communities have been described as egalitarian in nature. What is misleading about this description?

4. Explain the ways in which anthropologist Alan Kolata managed to reinvigorate farming practices among the Aymara.

5. It is said that "environments do not determine culture but do set certain potentials and limitations." Provide examples to support this statement.

6. What impact has intensive agriculture had on human society?

7. Describe the negative stereotype surrounding food foragers. How did it come about and why is it ill-founded?

SOLUTIONS

Fill-in-the-Blank

1. Adaptation
2. ecosystem
3. bison
4. farm
5. carrying
6. pastoral
7. food foraging
8. density of social relations
9. egalitarian
10. intensive agriculture

Chapter 5 ➤ *Making A Living*

11. 9,000
12. agriculture
13. horticulture
14. 60–70
15. meat
16. swidden

Multiple-Choice Practice Questions

1.	A	13.	B	25.	C
2.	E	14.	B	26.	C
3.	C	15.	D	27.	C
4.	C	16.	E	28.	D
5.	B	17.	D	29.	E
6.	D	18.	D	30.	E
7.	C	19.	B	31.	E
8.	E	20.	E	32.	D
9.	C	21.	E	33.	C
10.	A	22.	B		
11.	B	23.	A		
12.	D	24.	D		

True/False Practice Questions

1.	T	8.	F	15.	F
2.	T	9.	T	16.	F
3.	T	10.	F	17.	F
4.	F	11.	F	18.	T
5.	T	12.	F	19.	F
6.	F	13.	T	20.	T
7.	T	14.	T		

Practice Matching

1. D
2. B
3. C
4. E
5. A

CHAPTER 6
ECONOMIC SYSTEMS

SYNOPSIS

Challenge Issues: How do anthropologists study economic systems? How do different societies organize their economic resources and labour? How and why are goods exchanged or redistributed? Focusing on the study of the economic systems of nonliterate, nonindustrial societies, within the context of the total culture, this chapter summarizes the concepts anthropologists have developed to compare the organization of productive resources across cultures. The authors describe the major ways of distributing goods and services through reciprocity, redistribution, and market exchange. This chapter also considers the relevance of anthropological understanding applied to this era of globalization.

CHAPTER OBJECTIVES

- economic anthropology
- resources
- distribution and exchange
- consumption
- economics, culture, and the world of business
- gender perspectives: women and economic development
- anthropology applied: anthropology and the world of business

KEY TERMS

balanced reciprocity
conspicuous consumption
consumption
economic system
generalized reciprocity
globalization
informal economy

Kula ring
levelling mechanism
marine transhumance
market exchange
money
negative reciprocity
potlatch

reciprocity
redistribution
silent trade
technology

EXERCISES

Review Questions

1. Why might it be misleading to apply contemporary economic theories to preindustrial non-Western societies?

2. Explain the importance of yam production among the Trobrianders.

3. Provide examples that refute the notion of a division of labour by gender.

Chapter 6 ➤ *Economic Systems*

4. Compare and contrast the three general patterns of the division of labour by gender.

5. What are the benefits of the division of labour by age?

6. How is land controlled in most preindustrial societies?

7. Differentiate between the use of tools in foraging, horticultural, and agricultural communities.

8. Distinguish between industrial and nonindustrial societies with regard to craft specialization.

9. What is *marine transhumance* and how was the practice affected by resource depletion?

10. How do societies cooperate in the acquisition of food?

11. Describe the "myth of the squandering squatter" and explain how two constants found within "skid row" economy govern all exchange related behaviour.

12. Provide some examples of levelling mechanisms.

13. Distinguish between market exchange and marketplace.

14. What are three systems of exchange?

15. What purpose does reciprocity serve?

16. Differentiate between general, balanced, and negative reciprocity.

17. How is trade between groups generally conducted?

18. What were the primary contributions of Jomo Kenyatta?

19. What functions does the Kula ring serve?

20. What is money?

21. Describe redistribution among the Inca.

22. Describe the "informal economy" of North America.

23. How is conspicuous consumption used?

24. Discuss the ways in which anthropological concepts can be applied usefully to international business relations.

25. What are the drawbacks of ethnocentric interpretations of other societies' economic systems?

26. Discuss the role that culture plays in defining the "wants and needs" of a people.

Fill-in-the-Blank

1. All societies have rules pertaining to three productive resources: _____, _____ , and _____ .
2. Division of labour by gender varies from very flexible to very rigid. Among foragers like the _____ , either sex may do the work of the other without loss of face.
3. When two or more partners from different groups negotiate a direct exchange of one trade good for another, it is called_____ .
4. In most societies the basic unit in which cooperation takes place is the _____ .
5. Among horticulturalists, tools that are typically used are the _____ ,_____ , and _____ .
6. A_____ spreads wealth around so that no one accumulates substantially more wealth than anyone else.
7. _____ was the first to carry out a scientific investigation of the Kula ring.
8. According to Karl Polanyi, all forms of human exchange can be classified into three modes: _____, _____, and _____ .
9. The taxation systems of Canada and the United States are examples of _____ .
10. In some societies the surplus is used as a display for purposes of prestige. This is called _____ .
11. A(n) _____ is a network of producing and circulating marketable commodities, labour, and services that escape government control.

Chapter 6 ➤ *Economic Systems*

Multiple-Choice Practice Questions

1. When a man works hard in his horticultural garden in the Trobriand Islands to produce yams, he does this to satisfy which of the following demands?
   a. to have food for his household to eat
   b. to gain prestige by giving yams away to his sisters' husbands
   c. to prove to his wife that he can work as hard as she can
   d. to give the yams to his wife so that she can trade them for goods that they don't produce themselves
   e. to trade for fish

2. The productive resources used by all societies to produce goods and services include:
   a. raw materials
   b. labour
   c. technology
   d. bureaucrats
   e. raw materials, labour and technology

3. Among the First Nations, the traditional sexual division of labour falls into which pattern?
   a. flexible
   b. rigid segregation
   c. segregation with equality
   d. roll-reversible
   e. competitive

4. Among the Ju/'hoansi, _____.
   a. children are expected to contribute to subsistence from the time they are seven or eight
   b. elderly people past the age of sixty are expected to contribute hunted or gathered food to the group
   c. elderly people are a valuable source of knowledge and wisdom about hunting and gathering
   d. elderly people are taken care of grudgingly because after the age of sixty they contribute nothing to the group
   e. children are expected to set up their own separate households by the time they are twelve

5. In many nonindustrial societies, _____ .
   a. people prefer to have fun rather than to work
   b. cooperative work is usually done with a festive, sociable air
   c. cooperative work is always done in the household
   d. cooperative work groups are organized primarily for profit
   e. solitary work is preferred to cooperative work

6. Among food foragers such as the Ju/'hoansi, _____ .
   a. land is defined as a territory with usable resources and flexible boundaries that belongs to a band that has occupied it for a long time
   b. land is thought of as belonging to those who have bought it
   c. land is considered private property and access to the land can be denied
   d. land has clear-cut boundaries marked by survey posts
   e. land is controlled by a corporation of strangers

7. In nonindustrial societies, when a tool is complex and difficult to make it is usually considered to be owned by _____ .
   a. the whole village in which it is used
   b. a single individual
   c. the state
   d. all those who touch it
   e. all relatives

8. Levelling mechanisms_____.
   a. are more common in hunter-gatherer societies than in agricultural communities
   b. result in one family becoming wealthier than others
   c. are found in communities where property must not be allowed to threaten an egalitarian social order
   d. are more common in industrial societies than in agricultural societies
   e. no longer exist

9. The mode of distribution called reciprocity refers to the exchange of goods and services _____ .
   a. of unequal value
   b. between persons in hierarchical relationships
   c. for the purpose of maintaining social relationships and gaining prestige
   d. to make a profit
   e. to embarrass the person who gave the least

10. This type of exchange is likely the earliest form of human economic organization, according to Christopher Hauch.
   a. generalized reciprocity
   b. balanced reciprocity
   c. negative reciprocity
   d. silent trade
   e. redistribution

11. The Kula ring _____ .
   a. is a marriage ring made of shells
   b. is found among the Ju/'hoansi
   c. is found among the Andaman Islanders
   d. is a circular trade route along which various goods flow
   e. is a form of silent trade

12. The Canadian system of paying income taxes every April is an example of _____ .
   a. generalized reciprocity
   b. balanced reciprocity
   c. negative reciprocity
   d. redistribution
   e. market exchange

Chapter 6 ➤ *Economic Systems*

13. The display of wealth for social prestige is called _____.
    a. a levelling mechanism
    b. conspicuous consumption
    c. redistribution
    d. balanced reciprocity
    e. barter

14. Formal market exchange is usually associated with _____ .
    a. hunting and gathering bands
    b. horticultural tribes
    c. pastoral tribes
    d. a state type of political organization
    e. the household as the unit of production and consumption

15. A businessperson who wants to build a factory in the Middle East could benefit from the contributions of a cultural anthropologist. In which of the following ways would an anthropologist be likely to help?
    a. provide knowledge of the principles of market exchange
    b. introduce a new method of paying local workers
    c. tell the businessperson how to sit, dress, and talk when making the arrangements with local people
    d. screen workers who have diseases
    e. "introduce a new method of paying local workers" and "tell the businessperson how to sit, dress, and talk when making the arrangements with local people"

16. Silent trade is a specialized form of _____.
    a. informal economy
    b. barter
    c. prestige economy
    d. conspicuous consumption
    e. money

17. *Potlach* is an example of what type of practice?
    a. reciprocity
    b. silent trade
    c. conspicuous consumption
    d. negative reciprocity
    e. market exchange

18. Not only have anthropologists found niches for themselves in the world of business, but since 1972 the number of them going into business has grown _____ .
    a. tenfold
    b. fivefold
    c. 50 percent
    d. 1000 percent
    e. 25 percent

19. Victor Barac, a Canadian anthropologist, has provided valuable research for a variety of companies, with his two main areas of work, market research and _____.
    a. survey questionnaire
    b. corporate culture
    c. empirical science
    d. buzz factors
    e. public relations

20. The Inca Empire was known for practicing _____.
    a. generalized reciprocity
    b. balanced reciprocity
    c. negative reciprocity
    d. redistribution
    e. conspicuous consumption

21. In nonindustrial societies, land is often controlled by _____.
    a. individuals
    b. government by the state
    c. kinship groups
    d. a democratically elected political group
    e. none of the above

22. Which of the following was a form of money for the Aztecs?
    a. feathers
    b. salt
    c. yams
    d. cacao
    e. coconuts

23. An anthropologist interested in the systems of production, exchange, and redistribution would be called a(n) _____ anthropologist.
    a. political
    b. linguistic
    c. economic
    d. physical
    e. psychological

24. The division of labour by gender that has been described as the flexible/integrated pattern is found among which of the following?
    a. Bakhtiari
    b. Ju/'hoansi
    c. Taiwanese
    d. Dahomeans
    e. industrial countries

Chapter 6 ➤ *Economic Systems*

25. One example of specialization is afforded by the _____ people of Ethiopia's Danakil Depression. The men of this group are miners of salt.
    a. Nuer
    b. Azande
    c. Hadza
    d. Afar
    e. Ashanti

26. A societal obligation compelling a family to distribute goods so that no one accumulates more wealth than anyone else is referred to by anthropologists as a _____ .
    a. flat tax
    b. commune
    c. capital gains tax
    d. poverty spreader
    e. levelling mechanism

27. In economic anthropology, a mode of exchange in which the value of the gift is not calculated, nor is the time of repayment specified is known as _____ .
    a. charity
    b. generosity
    c. a handout
    d. generalized reciprocity
    e. Christmas

28. This anthropologist spent much of his career researching social and economic development in the Canadian north, with his unique style of dialogue between developers and aboriginal groups now serving as a model for planning and development in many parts of the world.
    a. Victor Barac
    b. Bruce Trigger
    c. Bronislaw Malinowski
    d. Richard Salisbury
    e. Jomo Kenyatta

29. Not all trade is motivated by economic considerations. A classic instance of this is _____ .
    a. silent trade
    b. the swap meet
    c. the flea market
    d. the Kula ring
    e. the *cargo* system

30. Among the _____ , both cacao beans and cotton cloaks served as money.
    a. Tiv
    b. Aztecs
    c. Enga
    d. Trobriand Islanders
    e. Inca

31. The Kula ring is a form of _____ that reinforces trade relations among a group of seafaring Melanesians inhabiting a ring of islands off the eastern coast of Papua New Guinea.
    a. negative reciprocity
    b. balanced reciprocity
    c. market exchange
    d. silent trade
    e. generalized reciprocity

32. _____ started as an anthropologist and later became the head of a national government.
    a. Franz Boas
    b. Gordon Childe
    c. Jomo Kenyatta
    d. Bruce Trigger
    e. A. R. Radcliffe-Brown

33. In the 30-year period following World War II, the cod population declined by _____ percent. This forced the Canadian government to place a temporary moratorium on northern cod, causing the fishing industry in Newfoundland and throughout Canada to collapse.
    a. 55
    b. 67
    c. 89
    d. 91
    e. 99

34. Christopher Hauch's study "Reciprocity on Skid Row" suggested that the causes of poverty on skid row are _____.
    a. almost always material and ordinary
    b an example of the "culture of poverty" model.
    c. a result of binge spending
    d. all of the above
    e. none of the above

35. Hauch`s study compares those living on skid row to _____.
    a. horticulturalists
    b. pastoralists
    c. foraging societies
    d. intensive agriculturalists
    e. none of the above

True/False Practice Questions

1. The Trobriands are in South America.
   True or False

2. In "silent trade," no words are spoken, but the participants must meet face to face to exchange goods.
   True or False

3. The Inca empire of Peru featured a highly efficient redistributive system.
   True or False

Chapter 6 ➤ *Economic Systems*

4. The number and kind of tools a society uses are related to its lifestyle.
   True or False

5. In the integrated pattern of labour, men and women carry out their work separately.
   True or False

6. Jomo Kenyatta was an anthropologist who became "the father" of modern Kenya.
   True or False

7. In societies without a money economy, the rewards of labour are never direct.
   True or False

8. There are three modes of redistribution.
   True or False

9. Anthropologists only work in exotic, faraway places like remote islands, deep forests, hostile deserts, or arctic wastelands.
   True or False

10. There is a potential job market for anthropologists in the market-research and design area.
    True or False

11. Individuals living on skid row can be compared to pastoral societies.
    True or False

12. Doing research in corporate America is not so different from doing initial anthropological research in an unfamiliar culture.
    True or False

13. Trobriand Island men devote a great deal of time and energy to raise yams, not for themselves but to give to others.
    True or False

14. No specialization of labour craft exists in nonindustrial societies.
    True or False

15. Anthropologists have found no form of conspicuous consumption occurring in nonindustrial societies.
    True or False

16. In non-Western societies the market is an important focus of social as well as economic activity.
    True or False

17. In Africa, much of the farming is the job of women. Failure to accept this fact is responsible for the failure of many development schemes, since outside experts design projects that usually assume the men in society are the farmers.
    True or False

18. The Kula ring used to involve thousands of men but no longer functions today.
    True or False

19. Anthropological research methods work well when conducting cross-cultural research, but are worthless in studying the modern corporate way of life.
    True or False

20. Canadian sanctions on cod fishing only affected fishing communities in Newfoundland.
    True or False

Practice Short Answer Questions

1. Describe and discuss the new form of market exchange that has developed in industrial and post-industrial societies.

2. Christopher Hauch describes "drunken binges as shrewd investments." Explain the meaning of this statement.

3. Describe and provide examples of each of the three forms of reciprocity.

4. How does the Inca Empire exhibit redistribution?

5. Compare and contrast levelling mechanism and prestige economy.

6. What is an informal economy?

7. Describe the economic system of the Ju/'hoansi.

Practice Essays

1. Compare and contrast the different ideas about the nature and control of land that exist among food foragers, horticulturalists, pastoralists, intensive agriculturalists, and industrialists.

2. Compare and contrast the different ideas about tools and tool ownership in foraging, horticultural, and intensive agricultural societies.

3. Describe what an anthropologist can contribute to the world of business.

4. Discuss the ways in which Christopher Hauch's research challenges some long-held assumptions about poverty and homelessness.

5. Specify and elaborate on the three categories of distribution of material goods.

6. What is money? What impact did its introduction have on culture?

7. What is *potlatch*? Discuss the history, meaning, and anthropological significance of the *potlach*.

8. Describe the contributions of Chinese-Canadians to the Canadian economy. Provide examples from the textbook.

Chapter 6 ➤ Economic Systems

9. Describe some of the problems that can occur when attempting to apply a Western development scheme to "underdeveloped" countries.

10. What is globalization? Describe the driving forces behind this phenomenon, as well as its effects.

11. Because trade can be essential in the quest for survival and is often undertaken for the sake of luxury, people may go to great lengths to establish and maintain good trade relations. A classic example of this is the Kula ring. What is the Kula ring? Describe.

12. Drawing on case studies and examples from your text, describe three diverse ways in which women have participated in economic development.

SOLUTIONS

Fill-in-the-Blank

1. production, exchange, redistribution
2. Ju/'hoansi
3. barter
4. household
5. axe, machete, hoe
6. levelling mechanism
7. Bronislaw Malinowski
8. reciprocity, redistribution, market exchange
9. redistribution
10. conspicuous consumption
11. informal economy

Multiple-Choice Practice Questions

1.	B	13.	B	25.	D
2.	E	14.	D	26.	E
3.	C	15.	E	27.	D
4.	C	16.	B	28.	D
5.	B	17.	C	29.	D
6.	A	18.	B	30.	B
7.	B	19.	D	31.	B
8.	C	20.	D	32.	C
9.	C	21.	C	33.	E
10.	A	22.	D	34.	A
11.	D	23.	C	35.	C
12.	D	24.	B		

True/False Practice Questions

1. F
2. F
3. T
4. T
5. F
6. T
7. F
8. F
9. F
10. T
11. F
12. T
13. T
14. F
15. F
16. T
17. T
18. F
19. F
20. F

CHAPTER 7
SEX AND MARRIAGE

SYNOPSIS

Challenge Issues: What is marriage? How is human sexuality viewed and controlled? Why is marriage universal? This chapter defines marriage as a system for regulating sexual access and explores varieties of marriage throughout the world. This chapter also considers and explores the great range of cultural variation in the way human sexuality is viewed, practised and controlled. Furthermore, this chapter explores some of the concerns surrounding certain practices, such as female circumcision, of which human rights and feminists groups have been vocal opponents.

CHAPTER OBJECTIVES

- human sexuality
- control of sexual relations
- anthropology applied: anthropology and the sex trade
- gender perspectives: female circumcision
- forms of marriage
- arranging marriage in India
- divorce

KEY TERMS

affinal kin	genetic explanation	polyandry
bride service	group marriage	polygamy
conjugal bond	incest taboo	polygyny
consanguineal kin	instinct explanation	psychoanalytical explanation
cooperation explanation	levirate	serial monogamy
dowry	marriage	sexual identity
endogamy	matrilateral cross-cousin marriage	sexual orientation
exogamy	monogamy	social explanation
female circumcision	patrilateral cross-cousin marriage	sororate

EXERCISES

Review Questions

1. With reference to examples from your textbook, describe some ways in which human sexuality is culturally constructed?

2. Why does sexual activity require social control?

3. Describe the sex life of the Trobrianders.

4. As discussed in your textbook, describe the traditional marriage system of the Nayar.

5. What is the incest taboo?

6. Describe the three main cultural reasons for the practice of female circumcision.

7. How are the changing societal views of homosexuality an interesting example of culture change in action?

8. How have geneticists, anthropologists, and psychologists attempted to explain the incest taboo?

9. Distinguish between endogamy and exogamy.

10. What were the initial reasons for exogamy, according to Levi-Strauss?

11. Distinguish between marriage and mating.

12. To what extent can North American society be characterized as monogamous?

13. Provide a non-ethnocentric definition of marriage.

14. Distinguish between polygynous and polyandrous families.

15. What form of marriage does the majority of the world's societies exhibit?

16. Characterize the typical polygynous society.

17. The Nandi of western Kenya occasionally engage in same-sex marriage. Explain when and why these types of marriage occur.

18. Describe the social and economic context of polyandry.

Chapter 7 ➤ *Sex and Marriage*

19. Discuss the contexts in which sororate, levirate, and serial monogamy are likely to occur.

20. What benefits do arranged marriages have?

21. Distinguish between patrilateral parallel-cousin and matrilateral cross-cousin marriage.

22. Distinguish between bride price, dowry, and bride service.

Fill-in-the-Blank

1. Marriage is a cultural transaction that regulates men's and women's rights of _____ access to one another and defines the context in which women are eligible to bear children.

2. _____ is a form of marriage in which a man or a woman marries or lives with a series of partners in succession.

3. Only about _____ percent of the world's societies prohibit all sexual involvement outside of marriage.

4. The bond between two individuals joined by marriage is called a(n) _____ bond.

5. "Blood" relatives, that is, relatives related by birth, are called _____ kin.

6. The _____ taboo prohibits sexual relations between specified individuals.

7. _____ is a rule mandating the one marry outside of a particular group, while _____ mandates marriage within the group.

8. In Canada, _____ is the only legally recognized form of marriage.

9. A _____ family contains a husband and his multiple wives, while a _____ family contains a wife and her multiple husbands.

10. The practice and study of female circumcision presents an _____ dilemma for many anthropologists.

11. When the wives in a polygynous marriage are sisters, this is called _____ polygyny.

12. _____ marriage refers to a marriage in which several men and women have sexual access to one another.

13. In a _____ , a widow marries the brother of her deceased husband; in a _____, a widower marries the sister of his deceased wife.

14. Marrying a sequence of partners throughout one's life is called _____ .

15. In a patrilateral parallel-cousin marriage, a boy marries his father's _____ daughter.

16. _____ is a gift exchange occurring at marriage in which money or goods are transferred from the groom's side to the bride's.

17. In a _____ system, the bride's family provides money or goods at the time of marriage.

18. The Nandi of western Kenya practice a form of marriage in which a woman marries a _____ .

19. The work by anthropologist _____ on female circumcision is regarded to be an insightful and balanced interpretation of a very difficult and challenging gender-focused issue.

20. _____ marriages are often preferred among some ethnic groups, such as East Indians, as a means of preserving traditional values.

Multiple-Choice Practice Questions

1. _____ is a transaction in which a woman and man establish a continuing claim to the right of sexual access to one another, and in which the woman involved becomes eligible to bear children.
   a. family
   b. marriage
   c. incest
   d. affinity
   e. sex

2. In which of the following countries is same-sex marriage considered socially acceptable and allowed by law?
   a. Mexico
   b. Canada
   c. Italy
   d. the Netherlands
   e. b and d

3. Marriage resolves the problem of how to bring sexual activity under _____ control.
   a. biological
   b. male
   c. cultural
   d. female
   e. mother-in-law

4. A household composed of married people contains _____ kin.
   a. affinal
   b. consanguineal
   c. endogamous
   d. nuclear
   e. instinctive

5. Only a minority of known societies, about _____ percent, have rules requiring that sexual involvement take place only within marriage.
   a. 25
   b. 15
   c. 10
   d. 5
   e. 30

Chapter 7 ➤ *Sex and Marriage*

6. Although all societies have some kind of incest taboo, the relationship that is considered incestuous may vary. Concepts of incest seem to be related to a group's definitions of endogamy and exogamy, thus suggesting that incest taboos may help to promote _____.
    a. alliances between groups
    b. inbreeding
    c. brother-sister marriages
    d. parallel-cousin marriages
    e. cross-cousin marriages

7. Marriage within a particular group of individuals is called _____.
    a. incest
    b. exogamy
    c. monogamy
    d. endogamy
    e. polygamy

8. The French anthropologist Claude Levi-Strauss says that the incest taboo is universal because humans _____.
    a. are instinctively opposed to inbreeding
    b. repress their sexual desire for the parent of the opposite sex
    c. have learned to establish alliances with strangers and thereby share and develop culture
    d. prefer to marry their brothers and sisters
    e. do not like sex

9. Which of the following *is not* an explanation for cross-culturally valid incest taboos?
    a. endogamy explanation
    b. psychoanalytical explanation
    c. genetic explanation
    d. social explanation
    e. instinct explanation

10. In some societies, preferred marriages are a man marrying his father's brother's daughter. This is known as patrilateral parallel-cousin marriage. Although not obligatory, such marriages have been favoured historically among which of the following cultures?
    a. traditional Chinese
    b. Arabs
    c. ancient Greece
    d. ancient Israelites
    e. traditional Chinese, Arabs, ancient Greece and ancient Israelites

11. _____ was a preferred form of marriage ranging from foragers (Australian Aborigines and the Haida) to intensive agriculturalist peoples of South India.
    a. patrilateral-cousin
    b. matrilateral cross-cousin
    c. polyandry
    d. polygamy
    e. levirate

12. Polygyny _____.
    a. means marriage to more than one man
    b. is the most common form of marriage
    c. is usually possible only when a man is fairly wealthy
    d. is less common than polyandry
    e. is an example of group marriage

13. An example of group marriage would be _____.
    a. a pastoral nomad's wife among the Turkana who actively searches for another woman to share her husband and her work with the livestock
    b. the Moonies having a large wedding ceremony at which five hundred couples, each one assigned to another, are married at the same time
    c. a prosperous member of the Kapauku in western New Guinea who is able to afford a bride price for four wives
    d. a hippy commune on a Gulf Island in British Columbia in which it is accepted that all adult members of the commune have sexual access to each other
    e. a Nayar household in which a woman takes several lovers

14. The levirate and the sororate_____ .
    a. are secret societies, like sororities and fraternities.
    b. function to maintain the relationship between the family of the bride and the family of the groom.
    c. are usually possible only when the man is fairly wealthy
    d. are types of cattle in pastoralist societies
    e. exist only in advanced industrial societies

15. Serial monogamy tends to occur in societies where _____ .
    a. a woman with children receives a great deal of help from her mother and brothers
    b. women do not have many children
    c. a woman with dependent children, isolated from her parents, marries a series of partners to get the assistance of another adult
    d. women are very wealthy
    e. divorce is forbidden

16. The main function of a bride price is _____ .
    a. for a man to show off to his wife how rich he is
    b. for a man to buy a slave
    c. for the wife's people to gain prestige in the village
    d. to compensate the wife's family for her labour
    e. for the wife's people to buy a husband for their daughter

17. When a man marries his father's brother's daughter in ancient Greece or traditional China, he
    a. is committing incest
    b. is practicing matrilineal cross-cousin marriage
    c. is practicing patrilateral parallel-cousin marriage
    d. is keeping property within the single male line of descent
    e. "is practicing patrilateral parallel-cousin marriage" and "he is keeping property within the single male line of descent"

Chapter 7 ➤ _Sex and Marriage_

18. In which of the following situations would you expect to find the custom of bride price?
    a. a bride and groom leave the community after marriage and set up their own household in a distant city
    b. a bride and groom go to live with the bride's people
    c. a bride and groom go to live with the groom's people
    d. a bride and groom go to live with the bride's mother's brother
    e. none of these

19. When the economy is based on_____ and where the man does most of the productive work, the bride's people may give a dowry that protects the woman against desertion and is a statement of her economic status.
    a. food foraging
    b. pastoralism
    c. intensive agriculture
    d. horticulture
    e. industrialism

20. The woman/woman marriage custom found in sub-Saharan Africa_____.
    a. enables a woman without sons to inherit a share of her husband's property
    b. confers legitimacy on the children of a woman who had been unable to find a husband
    c. enables the woman who adopts a male identity to raise her status
    d. enables the woman who is the wife of the female husband to raise her status and live a more secure life
    e. all of the above

21. Among the Gusii, which of the following constitutes a culturally valid reason for divorce?
    a. sterility or impotence
    b. cruelty
    c. being a poor provider
    d. being a lazy housekeeper
    e. all of the above

22. Which one of the following provinces does not legally recognize same-sex marriage?
    a. Ontario
    b. Quebec
    c. British Columbia
    d. Alberta
    e. Nova Scotia

23. According to the article in your textbook "Arranging Marriage in India," among urban Indians an important source of contacts in trying to arrange a marriage is/are the _____ .
    a. social club
    b. newspaper personals
    c. internet chat rooms
    d. matchmaking businesses
    e. Temple

24. Which of the following characteristics would be most important in an Indian family's selection of a bride for their son?
    a. good looks
    b. well-educated
    c. independent
    d. have higher social status
    e. good character

25. _____has gained an international reputation for research into the meaning of various ritual practices, such as female circumcision.
    a. Bronislaw Malinowski
    b. Janice Boddy
    c. Claude Levi-Strauss
    d. Phillipe Cousteau
    e. Emile Durkheim

26. It has been noted that _____ , much like humans, tend to avoid breeding with siblings, suggesting that the tendency for humans to look for sexual partners outside the group they have been raised in is not just the result of a cultural taboo.
    a. chimpanzees
    b. bonobos
    c. macaques
    d. orangutans
    e. gorillas

27. Currently, close to _____ percent first marriages in Canada end in divorce.
    a. 13
    b. 20
    c. 27
    d. 31
    e. 40

28. A(n)_____ family is established through marriage.
    a. nuclear
    b. extended
    c. affinal
    d. consanguineal
    e. conjugal

29. The *Tali-tying* ceremony and *sambandham* are associated with the _____of southwest India.
    a. Nandi
    b. Nayar
    c. Azande
    d. Mundugamor
    e. Kikuyu

Chapter 7 ➤ *Sex and Marriage*

30. _____marriage is when several men and women have sexual access to one another.
    a. fictive
    b. group
    c. affinal
    d. conjugal
    e. non-traditional

31. In Canada, as in most Western countries, _____ is the only legally recognized
    form of marriage.
    a. polygamy
    b. polygyny
    c. monogamy
    d. polyandry
    e. serial

32. Most divorced people in Canada remarry at least once. Thus, _____ is
    not uncommon.
    a. polygamy
    b. serial monogamy
    c. sororate marriage
    d. levirate marriage
    e. polyandry

33. Conjugal families are formed on the basis of marital ties between husband and wife. Which of the
    following are forms of conjugal families?
    a. polyandrous families
    b. consanguine families
    c. polygynous families
    d. nuclear families
    e. polyandrous families, polygynous families, and nuclear families

34. In some societies, when a woman marries she receives her share of the family inheritance, or her
    _____ .
    a. bride price
    b. bride service
    c. dowry
    d. bride commission
    e. birthright

35. _____ has an insider's perspective with regards to female circumcision, as
    she was circumcised during initiation into a secret women's society in Sierra Leone.
    a. Janice Boddy
    b. Mary Daly
    c. Fuambai Ahmadu
    d. Margaret Mead
    e. none of the above

True/False Practice Questions

1. Trobriand children begin sexual experimentation at a young age.
   True or False

2. About half of the world's societies prohibit sexual involvement outside of marriage.
   True or False

3. There is only one type of family.
   True or False

4. Brother-sister marriages were common among farmers in Roman Egypt.
   True or False

5. In a polygamy union, the couple goes to live with the husband's mother's family.
   True or False

6. People want pretty much the same things in marriage whether it is in India or America.
   True or False

7. Today, a dowry is expected by law in India.
   True or False

8. In India it is understood that matches (marriages) would be arranged only within the same caste and general social class.
   True or False

9. In India no crossing of subcastes is permissible even if the class positions of the bride's and groom's families are similar.
   True or False

10. As far as arranging a marriage is concerned, in India the basic rule seems to be that a family's reputation is most important.
    True or False

11. Young men of the Tlingit, living on the northwest coast of British Columbia and south-eastern Alaska, traditionally preferred matrilateral cross-cousin marriage.
    True or False

12. Same-sex marriage has only been observed in North America and Europe.
    True or False

13. Extended families are rare.
    True or False

14. Group marriage is legal in some parts of Canada.
    True or False

15. Bronislaw Malinowski put forth the *social explanation* as a justification for incest taboos.
    True or False

Chapter 7 ➤ Sex and Marriage

16. Divorce is possible in all societies, though reasons for divorce as well as its frequency vary widely from one society to another.
True or False

17. Female circumcision is a ritual practice found in most African cultures.
True or False

18. Chimpanzees do not engage in sexual relations with their siblings.
True or False

19. Both cross-cultural studies and those of other animals suggest that homosexual behaviour is unnatural.
True or False

20. A number of Canadian provinces and European countries recognize the legality of same-sex marriage.
True or False

Practice Matching

Match the culture with its characteristic.

1.	_____	Nandi
2.	_____	Aborigines of Australia
3.	_____	Nayar
4.	_____	Tibetans
5.	_____	North Americans

a. a culture emphasizing love and choice as a basis for marriage
b. South Indian people who give the mother's brothers key responsibility in child rearing
c. a group that favours matrilateral cross-cousin marriage
d. East African pastoralists who practice woman/woman marriage
e. polyandrous society of central Asia

Short Answer Practice Questions

1. What is the positive outcome of having strict religious rules that regulate sexual relations?

2. Explain why your textbook's definition of marriage refers to "persons" rather than "a man and a woman."

3. Describe the various forms of residence pattern.

4. Who is Pamela Downe and what was her research focus?

5. Distinguish between matrilateral and patrilateral cross-cousin marriages.

6. What is the difference between marriage and mating?

7. Describe some of the possible explanations for female circumcision.

_94_   _Chapter 7_ ➤ _Sex and Marriage_

8. What are some of the reasons for arranged marriages in India?

9. Explain the incest taboo.

Practice Essays

1. Discuss how various societies have sought to regulate sexual relations.

2. Explain the universality of the incest taboo and describe its cross-cultural variation. Also consider and discuss the five possible explanations for the incest taboo.

3. Discuss Pamela Downe's research among women working in the sex trade. How was Downe able to provide a conduit for the voices of sex trade workers?

4. What factors affect the stability of marriages and the choice of mates?

5. What factors must be taken into consideration when arranging a marriage in India? Describe.

6. Describe the Nayar and their rules of sexual access.

7. Anthropologists have found that universally societies have cultural rules that act to control sexual relations. What are the rules of sexual access from one culture to another?

8. Define sexual orientation and sexual identity and clarify the distinction between both terms.

9. Expound on the reasons and frequency of divorce from society to society.

10. Give an account of the history of views toward homosexuality and consider the ways in which it has and has not been accepted as a sexual practice and lifestyle.

SOLUTIONS

Fill-in-the-Blank

1. sexual
2. serial monogamy
3. five
4. conjugal
5. consanguineal
6. incest
7. exogamy, endogamy
8. monogamy
9. polygynous, polyandrous
10. ethical
11. sororal
12. group
13. levirate, sororate
14. serial marriage

Chapter 7 ➤ Sex and Marriage

15. brother's
16. bride price
17. dowry
18. woman
19. Janice Boddy
20. arranged

Multiple-Choice Practice Questions

1.	B	13.	D	25.	B
2.	E	14.	B	26.	A
3.	C	15.	C	27.	E
4.	A	16.	D	28.	E
5.	D	17.	E	29.	B
6.	A	18.	C	30.	B
7.	D	19.	C	31.	C
8.	C	20.	E	32.	B
9.	A	21.	A	33.	E
10.	E	22.	D	34.	C
11.	B	23.	A	35.	C
12.	C	24.	E		

True/False Practice Questions

1.	T	8.	T	15.	T
2.	F	9.	F	16.	T
3.	F	10.	T	17.	F
4.	T	11.	F	18.	T
5.	F	12.	F	19.	F
6.	F	13.	F	20.	T
7.	F	14.	F		

Practice Matching

1. D
2. C
3. B
4. E
5. A

CHAPTER 8
FAMILY AND HOUSEHOLD

SYNOPSIS

Challenge Issues: What is the family? How can it be defined? What is the difference between family and household and what are some of the problems of family and household organizations? This chapter focuses on how culture is transmitted from one generation to the next and considers the various types of household and family units found worldwide. This chapter discusses the unstable, changing nature of the family structure in response to particular social, historical, and ecological circumstances.

CHAPTER OBJECTIVES

- the family defined
- how many fathers are best for a child
- functions of the family
- gender perspectives: the motherhood mandate
- family and household
- form of the family
- residence patterns
- problems of family and household organization
- anthropology applied: public health surveillance and First Nations self-government

KEY TERMS

ambilocal residence	family	nuclear family
avunculocal residence	fraternal polyandry	patrilocal residence
conjugal family	household	polyandrous family
consanguine family	matrilocal residence	polygynous family
extended family	neolocal residence	sororal polygyny

Exercises

Review Questions

1. Distinguish between consanguineal and conjugal families.

2. What is the household and how is it different from the family?

3. Why might North American children's development of self-awareness lag behind that of children from non-Western societies?

4. Who is Laurel Bossen? What is the focus of her research?

5. What is the nuclear family?

6. Describe the treatment of infants among the Ju/'hoansi.

7. What is the "motherhood mandate"?

8. Distinguish between dependence and independence training.

9. Distinguish between polyandrous and polygynous families.

10. What was the Nayar marriage system in traditional times?

11. What caused the nuclear family to become isolated from other kin in Europe and North America?

12. What is enculturation?

13. What is the economic incentive for a household to include members of both sexes?

14. Describe who may be included as part of the extended family. Is the extended family structure evident in Canada?

15. What are the two main categories of same-sex families?

16. Distinguish between patrilocal and matrilocal residence.

17. What is ambilocal residence?

18. Distinguish between sororal and fraternal polyandry.

19. Define family.

20. What type of family is characteristic of many nonindustrial societies?

Fill-in-the-Blank

1. The 1960s saw a number of attempts by young people in Canada and the United States to reinvent a form of extended family. These groups of unrelated nuclear families living together were known as _____.

2. The term _____ refers to the process by which culture is transmitted from one generation to the next.

3. In traditional times, the Nayar marriage system served to maintain a _____ family.

4. Anthropologist _____ discovered that paternity among the Bari' Indians in Venezuela is understood to be very flexible.

5. In a 1981 article titled_____ by C. Owen Lovejoy, humans are presented as naturally monogamous.

6. The Na of Yunnan Province in China have a _____ -centric society in which husbands are not part of the picture.

7. Generally, _____ families are most apt to be found in cultures with an economy based on subsistence farming.

8. Same-sex families can be divided into two main categories: stepfamilies and _____ families.

9. A woman goes to live with her husband in the household he grew up in: this is called _____ residence.

10. _____ residence is common among foraging people.

Multiple-Choice Practice Questions

1. In an ambilocal residence pattern,
    a. a married couple live in the locality of the husband's family
    b. a married couple live in the locality of the wife's family
    c. a married couple live in the locality of neither the husband's nor the wife's family
    d. a married couple live in the locality of either the husband's or wife's family
    e. none of the above

2. The agents of enculturation_____.
    a. are persons involved in transmitting culture to the next generation
    b. are at first the members of the family into which the child is born
    c. vary, depending on the structure of the family into which a child is born
    d. include peer groups and schoolteachers
    e. "are persons involved in transmitting culture to the next generation," "are at first the members of the family into which the child is born," "vary, depending on the structure of the family into which a child is born," and "include peer groups and schoolteachers"

Chapter 8 ➤ *Family and Household*

3. Which of the following statements about self-awareness is *incorrect*?
   a. Self-awareness occurs earlier in children as a function of the amount of social stimulation they receive.
   b. At fifteen weeks of age, the home-reared infant in North America is in contact with its mother about 20 percent of time.
   c. At fifteen weeks of age, infants in Ju/'hoansi society are in close contact with their mothers about 70 percent of the time.
   d. American children develop self-awareness earlier than do Ju/'hoansi children.
   e. all of the above

4. Generally, the pattern of residence in industrial societies such as Canada is _____.
   a. neolocal
   b. avunculocal
   c. matrilocal
   d. patrilocal
   e. none of the above

5. A residential kin group composed of a married woman and man and their dependent children is best described as a/an _____.
   a. family
   b. conjugal bond
   c. endogamous
   d. nuclear family
   e. serial marriage

6. A woman with several husbands is a member of a _____ family.
   a. nuclear
   b. polygynous
   c. polyandrous
   d. serial
   e. conjugal

7. Select the *incorrect* statement about Inuit childrearing practices.
   a. Inuit infants are rarely left alone when awake.
   b. Inuit babies and small children receive a great deal of love and attention from their family.
   c. Inuit parents rarely become angry with their children.
   d. Inuit children tend to lag behind in the development of self-awareness compared to children raised in an industrial society.
   e. Mothers tend to nurse and hold their infants on demand, cuddling them most of the time.

8. Independence training is more likely in _____.
   a. small nuclear families
   b. large extended families
   c. small-scale horticultural societies where a man has many wives
   d. a pastoralist family where a woman has many husbands and the extended family has to be always on the move
   e. New York City neighbourhoods where large families stay nearby

9. Dependence training is more likely in _____ .
   a. nuclear families
   b. societies whose subsistence is based on pastoralism
   c. a food-foraging society
   d. extended families in societies whose economy is based on subsistence farming
   e. industrial societies

10. A living arrangement in which the children live with their mothers, apart from men until age 13, whereupon the boys leave to live with the village men is common to the _____.
    a. Bari' Indians
    b. Roman Catholics
    c. Inuit
    d. Ju/'hoansi
    e. Mundurucu

11. Among the Na of Yunnan Province in China, _____.
    a. women never marry or move away from the family compound
    b. male lovers are simply visitors
    c. there is no term that would cover the notion of father
    d. all of the above
    e. none of the above

12. What is the "motherhood mandate"?
    a. a rule book for mothers
    b. a theory, which suggests that women want to become mothers and have a deep-rooted "maternal instinct" that pushes her toward this goal
    c. an essay by Susan Basow
    d. "a theory, which suggests that women want to become mothers and have a deep-rooted 'maternal instinct' that pushes her toward this goal" and "an essay by Susan Basow"
    e. none of the above

13. Laurel Bossen, a Canadian anthropologist, studied among the_____, _____, and _____ for her early multi-cited ethnography "The Redivision of Labour" (1984).
    a. Guatemalan, Mayan, and Chinese
    b. Chinese, French, and Japanese
    c. Mayan, Guatemalan, and Hispanic
    d. Hispanic, Chinese, and African-American
    e. West Indies, Guatemalan, and Mayan

14. Although Trobriand leaders and chiefs lived avunculocally, most married couples in this society lived _____.
    a. matrilocally
    b. neolocally
    c. ambilocally
    d. avunculocally
    e. patrilocally

Chapter 8 ➤ *Family and Household*

15. In 2001, roughly _____ percent of Canadian families were "lone-parent" families.
   a. 12.7
   b. 13.2
   c. 15.6
   d. 21.4
   e. 17.3

16. _____ percent of "lone-family' households are headed by women.
   a. 47.2
   b. 51.9
   c. 62.7
   d. 76.8
   e. 81.3

17. In traditional times, _____ families of the Inuit exploited the vast Arctic wilderness for food.
   a. nuclear
   b. extended
   c. consanguineal
   d. same-sex
   e. none of the above

18. In_____ infants generally do not sleep with their parents, most often being put in rooms of their own. This is seen as an important step in making them into individuals, "owners" of themselves and their capacities, rather than part of some social whole.
   a. the Ituri rain forest
   b. China
   c. Canada
   d. Mexico
   e. the Kalahari Desert

19. The essay by _____ suggests that all "normal" women want to become mothers and women feel pressured to live up to the supermom media image.
   a. Laurel Bossen
   b. Karen Brodkin Sacks
   c. Deborah Tannen
   d. Susan Basow
   e. Laura Nader

20. The _____ is the basic residential unit where economic production, consumption, inheritance, childrearing, and shelter are organized and implemented.
   a. family
   b. home
   c. village
   d. household
   e. city

21. Today, Chinese-Canadian families may not carry on the tradition of the daughter-in-law caring for her husband's elderly parents because _____ .
    a. the daughter-in-law may work outside the home and cannot stay home to care for her in-laws
    b. many Chinese-Canadian seniors prefer to live apart from their children
    c. "the daughter-in-law may work outside the home" and "many Chinese-Canadian seniors prefer to live apart from their children"
    d. the daughter tends to have difficulty getting along with her in-laws
    e. none of the above

22. A commune is an example of a reinvented form of _____ family.
    a. matrilocal
    b. patrilocal
    c. extended
    d. nuclear
    e. neolocal

23. The development of self-awareness is part of the _____ process.
    a. biocultural
    b. enculturation
    c. familial
    d. sororal
    e. neolocal

24. All societies must somehow ensure that their culture is adequately transmitted from one generation to the next. This transmission process is _____ .
    a. acculturation
    b. assimilation
    c. enculturation
    d. absorption
    e. integration

25. Breast-fed children tend to _____ .
    a. have fewer allergies
    b. have fewer ear infections
    c. have less diarrhoea
    d. be at less risk of sudden infant death syndrome
    e. all of the above

True/False Practice Questions

1. The specific form that family takes is related to particular social, historical and ecological circumstances.
   True or False

2. Family and household are essentially synonymous terms.
   True or False

3. Industrial societies promote independence training in their mobile nuclear families.
   True or False

Chapter 8 ➤ Family and Household

4. Dependence training and the concept of "face" or "honour" are techniques to enforce harmony within extended families.
True or False

5. The Motherhood Mandate provides a guideline for how women can become supermoms.
True or False

6. The most prominent family group among the Inuit is the extended family.
True or False

7. Among the Mundurucu, the women and men live in separate areas of the village.
True or False

8. China's strict one child per household policy is proving problematic as the elderly have only one child to take care of them in their old age.
True or False

9. Children raised in same-sex families show no significant difference in development to children raised in families with heterosexual parents.
True or False

10. Laurel Bossen proved in her ethnographic research that gender relations do not differ based on ethnicity and class.
True or False

11. Among the Ju/'hoansi, infants are nursed up to 4 or 5 times an hour.
True or False

12. There is a belief among the Bari' that a child can have more than a single biological father.
True or False

13. In Canada, common-law families account for 50 percent of the families.
True or False

14. The roots of the traditional European nuclear family go back to a series of regulations the Roman Catholic Church imposed in the 4th century CE.
True or False

15. Children learn most of what they need to know through explicit verbal instruction.
True or False

16. Near-constant stimulation plays a key role in the "hardwiring" of the brain, as stimulation is necessary for the development of the neural circuitry.
True or False

17. In many foraging societies, children are raised by only their biological parents.
True or False

18. The most prevalent form of same-sex families are lesbian co-parent families.
True or False

19. A man leaving his family to live with his wife in her parents' household is involved in a patrilocal residence pattern.
True or False

20. Breast-feeding has proven health benefits for infants.
True or False

Short Answer Practice Questions

1. Who are the Bari' Indians and what is unique about their notion of biological paternity?

2. Why does self-awareness occur earlier among Ju/'hoansi and Inuit children?

3. Describe the following residence patterns: ambilocal, neolocal, and avunculocal.

4. How is jealousy and bickering kept to a minimum in polygynous families?

5. Outside of industrialized societies such as Canada, where are single-parent families common? Why?

Practice Essays

1. How has the Bari' notion of paternity challenged long-held assumptions about human mating behaviour?

2. What is the Motherhood Mandate? How are children socialized to become "good mothers"? How has the media provided us with unrealistic images of motherhood?

3. Discuss the parallels between the nuclear family in industrial societies and in families living under especially harsh environmental conditions.

4. Discuss the various types of extended families as explored in your textbook. How are they all considered to be extended families?

5. In North America, the vast majority of single-parent households are female-run. Why is this the case? What are some of the concerns and issues for these families?

6. Discuss the research project of John O'Neil, Joseph Kaufert, Pat Kaufert, and Kue Young. Why is it important for First Nations to gain control over technologies of public health surveillance?

7. Cai Hua writes, "I have not found any term that would cover the notion of father in the Na language." Explain this statement with reference to Na society.

8. Describe the fears expressed by some members of society surrounding same-sex families.

Chapter 8 ➤ _Family and Household_

Solutions

Fill-in-the-Blank

1. communes
2. enculturation
3. consanguine
4. Stephen Beckerman
5. The Origin of Man
6. female
7. extended
8. co-parent
9. patrilocal
10. ambilocal

Multiple-Choice Practice Questions

1. D
2. E
3. D
4. A
5. D
6. C
7. D
8. A
9. D
10. E
11. D
12. D
13. C
14. E
15. C
16. E
17. A
18. C
19. D
20. D
21. D
22. C
23. B
24. C
25. E

True/False Practice Questions

1. T
2. F.
3. T
4. T
5. F
6. F
7. T
8. T
9. T
10. F
11. T
12. T
13. F
14. T
15. F
16. T
17. F
18. F
19. F
20. T

CHAPTER 9
KINSHIP AND DESCENT

SYNOPSIS

Challenge Issues: What are descent groups? What functions do descent groups serve? How do descent groups form? This chapter presents key concepts relating to the anthropological study of kinship and descent, including the varieties of descent group and the organization and function of these groups as adaptive mechanisms. The chapter also includes a discussion of the relations between gender and kinship, as well as the political importance of descent for First Nations. Finally, this chapter considers kinship terminology and kinship groups.

CHAPTER OBJECTIVES

- why we study kinship
- urban kinship systems in Canada
- descent groups
- coping as a woman in a man's world
- gender perspectives: the kinkeepers
- forms and functions of descent groups
- applied anthropology: federal recognition for B.C. First Nations
- contemporary Chinese-Canadian Kinship
- kinship terminology and kinship groups

KEY TERMS

ambilineal descent	fission	moiety
clan	Hawaiian system	Omaha system
Crow system	Iroquois system	patrilineal descent
descent group	kindred	Sudanese (descriptive) system
double descent	kinship	totemism
Eskimo system	lineage	unilineal descent
fictive kinship	matrilineal descent	

EXERCISES

Review Questions

1. Why do societies form descent groups?

2. How is membership in a descent group restricted?

3. Distinguish between patrilineal and matrilineal descent groups.

Chapter 9 ➤ *Kinship and Descent*

4. What function does double descent serve?

5. What functions do descent groups serve?

6. How is a lineage reckoned?

7. What are the social implications of lineage exogamy?

8. Contrast a clan and a lineage.

9. What purpose do totems serve a clan?

10. What is a moiety?

11. How do bilateral systems differ from unilateral systems?

12. What are the functions and limitations of ego-centred groups?

13. Why do descent groups emerge?

14. What functions do kinship terminologies serve?

15. What are the major systems of kinship terminology?

16. What is the main feature of the Eskimo system of descent?

17. What is the simplest kinship system? Why is it considered simple?

18. With which type of descent group is Iroquois terminology commonly correlated?

19. How can anthropologists assist First Nations to establish rights and titles in court?

20. Distinguish between and describe the Crow and Omaha systems of descent.

Multiple-Choice Practice Questions

1. Descent groups _____ .
   a. are composed of those who claim to be lineally descended from a particular ancestor
   b. are common in human societies
   c. help provide jobs for their members
   d. all of the above
   e. none of the above

2. By tracing membership either through males or through females, members of unilineal descent groups _____ .
   a. know exactly to which group they belong and where their primary loyalties lie
   b. are confused about their relationship to persons not included in the group
   c. act like females if they are in a matrilineal group
   d. act like males if they are in a patrilineal group
   e. know exactly how many children they are going to have

3. You belong to a patrilineal descent group. Which of the following belong to the same group?
   a. your mother
   b. your father's sister
   c. your mother's sister
   d. your mother's father
   e. your father's sister's children

4. A network of relatives within which individuals possess certain mutual rights and obligations is called _____.
   a. exogamy
   b. descent
   c. kindred
   d. terminology
   e. kinship

5. A boy is born into a society that practices matrilineal descent. The person who exercises authority over him is _____.
   a. his sister
   b. his father
   c. his mother
   d. his mother's brother
   e. his father's sister

Chapter 9 ➤ *Kinship and Descent*

6. Among the Yako of Nigeria, an individual might inherit grazing lands from his father's patrilineal group, and livestock and ritual knowledge from his mother's matrilineal group. This is an example of _____ descent.
    a. ambilineal
    b. bilocal
    c. patrilateral
    d. indivisible
    e. double

7. Which of the following kinship terminology systems is most commonly found in Canada?
    a. Eskimo
    b. Hawaiian
    c. Iroquois
    d. Crow
    e. Omaha

8. Descent groups _____ .
    a. are economic units providing mutual aid
    b. provide social security for elderly members
    c. often promote solidarity by encouraging worship of the group's ancestors
    d. play a role in deciding appropriate marriage partners
    e. "are economic units providing mutual aid," "provide social security for elderly members," "often promote solidarity by encouraging worship of the group's ancestors," and "play a role in deciding appropriate marriage partners"

9. A lineage is a corporate descent group _____ .
    a. the members of which can buy shares in the corporation
    b. the members of which claim descent from a common ancestor
    c. the members of which know the exact genealogical linkages by which they are related to the common ancestor
    d. composed of consanguineal kin
    e. "the members of which claim descent from a common ancestor," "the members of which know the exact genealogical linkages by which they are related to the common ancestor," and "composed of consanguineal kin"

10. A totem _____.
    a. is central to the ways in which important families were divided among the Haida
    b. is a symbol of animals, plants, natural forces, and objects
    c. is usually associated with a clan's concept of its mythical origins
    d. all of the above
    e. none of the above

11. If the entire culture is divided into two major descent groups, each group is called a
    a. moiety
    b. totem
    c. kindred
    d. lineage
    e. clan

12. Members of a moiety _____ .
    a. believe they share a common ancestor, but cannot prove it through definite genealogical links.
    b. are those who are divorced (they lack their "better half")
    c. are usually able to trace their exact genealogical links to their common ancestor
    d. feel a much stronger feeling of kinship than is felt by members of a lineage or clan
    e. belong to a group that is smaller than a lineage

13. A person in a system of bilateral descent _____ .
    a. traces descent through the father for some purposes and through the mother for other purposes
    b. traces descent through female lines
    c. traces descent through male lines
    d. uses totems to symbolically represent the group
    e. traces descent through both parents simultaneously and recognizes multiple ancestors

14. Descent groups are frequently found to be important organizing devices in _____ .
    a. food-foraging societies
    b. horticultural societies
    c. pastoral societies
    d. intensive agricultural societies
    e. horticultural societies, pastoral societies and intensive agricultural societies

15. _____ develop out of extended families when families split up and move to nearby regions, and the core members of these families recognize their descent from a common ancestor and continue to organize activities based on this idea.
    a. phratries
    b. kindred groups
    c. lineages
    d. moieties
    e. cognatic groups

16. If two people are given the same kinship term, this means that _____ .
    a. they have the same genes
    b. no one can tell the difference between them
    c. they occupy a similar status
    d. they are identical twins
    e. they are members of an adopted family

17. In _____ kinship terminology, ego's "brother" and "sister" are distinguished from "cousins"; both ego's father's brother and mother's brother are given the same kinship term, "uncle."
    a. Eskimo
    b. Hawaiian
    c. Crow
    d. Omaha
    e. Iroquois

Chapter 9 ➤ Kinship and Descent

18. In the _____ system of kinship terminology, ego's father, father's brother, and mother's brother are all referred to by the same term, and ego's mother, mother's sister, and father's sister are all referred to by the same term; the term "brother" includes ego's brothers as well as male cousins.
    a. Iroquois
    b. Crow
    c. Omaha
    d. Hawaiian
    e. Eskimo

19. In _____ kinship terminology, the term "brother" is given to ego's brother, father's brother's son, and mother's sister's son; a different term is used for the sons of father's sister and mother's brother. "Mother" refers to ego's mother and mother's sister; "father" refers to ego's father and father's brother. Separate terms are used for ego's mother's brother and father's sister.
    a. Eskimo
    b. Hawaiian
    c. Iroquois
    d. cognatic
    e. kindred

20. Patrilineal descent is also called _____ .
    a. bilateral descent
    b. double descent
    c. matrilineal descent
    d. cognitive descent
    e. agnatic descent

21. Which of the following *is not* part of the "kinkeeper" role?
    a. maintaining formal and informal ties with other extended-family members
    b. sending cards or emails and acknowledging special events
    c. possessing a certain power over the family
    d. being a senior male
    e. being responsible for emotional support

22. Chinese immigrants in Canada organized their lives around _____, rather than the traditional system based on common residence and corporate property.
    a. common-interest associations
    b. clan associations
    c. district associations
    d. B and C
    e. A and C

23. _____ has observed the Ts'msyeen Nation as both a member and an anthropologist, and has utilized their anthropological knowledge to work with community members in order to understand the ways in which Ts'msyeen society is organized, in an effort to present that information to the Canadian courts and outsider institutions in a clear manner.
    a. Parin Dossa
    b. Margery Wolf
    c. Peggy Reeves Sanday
    d. A.R. Radcliffe-Brown
    e. Charles Menzies

24. This British anthropologist defined totemism.
    a. Margaret Mead
    b. Leslie White
    c. Julian Steward
    d. A. R. Radcliffe-Brown
    e. Geoffrey Gorer

25. Which of the following statements *does not* relate to or describe Parin Dossa's research:
    a. interested in documenting the richness of people's lives while critiquing domination and human inequality
    b. seeks to explore the question "What is social knowledge for?" using the narratives of Muslim women from the margins
    c. has examined the question of how anthropologists can theorize and learn from the "telling and listening paradigm"
    d. has done extensive ethnographic research among various First Nations groups in Canada
    e. has researched Muslim women in Canada and Kenya

26. All societies have found some form of family and/or household organization to be a convenient way to deal with problems all human groups encounter. Which of the following would be problems all human groups face?
    a. how to facilitate economic cooperation between the sexes
    b. when to retire
    c. how to regulate sexual activity
    d. how to provide a proper setting for child rearing
    e. "how to facilitate economic cooperation between the sexes," "how to regulate sexual activity," and "how to provide a proper setting for child rearing"

27. The Sudanese or descriptive system of kinship terminology has come to replace Iroquois terminology the among rural _____.
    a. Sudanese
    b. Anglo-Canadians
    c. Hawaiian
    d. Chinese
    e. Hopi

Chapter 9 ➤ *Kinship and Descent*

28. The kinship system in which each cousin is distinguished from all others, as well as siblings, and each uncle and aunt is potentially called by a separate kin term is known as the _____ .
    a. Crow system
    b. Hawaiian system
    c. Sudanese or descriptive system
    c. Eskimo system
    d. none of the above

29. The descent system that allows each individual the option of affiliating with either the mother's or the father's descent group is known as _____ descent.
    a. double
    b. matrilineal
    c. patrilineal
    d. avunculocal
    e. ambilineal

30. Which of the following groups is a matrilineal society?
    a. Yanomamo
    b. Chinese
    c. Hopi
    d. Iroquois
    e. Yako

31. Which of the following is *not* a lineage system?
    a. matrilineal
    b. patrilineal
    c. unilineal
    d. trifurcated
    e. bilateral

True/False Practice Questions

1. Cross-cousins are ideal marriage partners in an arrangement whereby lineages engage in reciprocal marriage exchanges to establish alliances.
    True or False

2. Ambilineal descent is a form of double descent.
    True or False

3. Only the Sudanese employ the Sudanese or descriptive kinship terminology system.
    True or False

4. The boundaries of a kindred are permanent and definite.
    True or False

5. Samoan Islanders practice unilineal descent.
    True or False

6. Totemism is defined as the use of totem poles in religious ceremony.
   True or False

7. Bilateral descent exists in various foraging cultures.
   True or False

8. All kinship terminologies classify similar individuals into similar categories.
   True or False

9. Euro-Americans commonly use the Iroquois system of kinship.
   True or False

10. One unintended consequence of Charles Menzie's lineage research among B.C. First Nations has been the production of local curriculum resources for use in local schools.
    True or False

11. Among the Hopi, residence is patrilocal.
    True or False

12. Ts'msyeen people continue to rely extensively upon their ability to fish, hunt, and gather food and other resources.
    True or False

13. Unilineal descent provides an easy way of restricting descent group membership to minimize problems of divided loyalty and the like.
    True or False

14. Bilateral kinship and bilateral descent cannot be used interchangeably since they have different meanings.
    True or False

15. Descent groups do not need to clearly define membership to operate efficiently.
    True or False

16. In a society where descent is traced patrilineally, maternal relatives are less important.
    True or False

17. Double descent, whereby descent is reckoned both patrilineally and matrilineally at the same time, is very rare.
    True or False

18. Because of its bilateral structure, a kindred is never the same for any two persons except siblings. Thus, no two people (except siblings) belong to the same kindred.
    True or False

Chapter 9 ➤ *Kinship and Descent*

Practice Short Answer Questions

1. Describe the social structure of the Ts'msyeen.

2. Who is Parin Dossa? What three theoretical and practice-based orientations guide her research?

3. What is a kinkeeper? What does this role involve?

4. Why do we study kinship?

5. Explain the difference between clan, lineage, and moiety.

6. How are women commonly stereotyped in rural Taiwan?

7. What are the differences between a matrilineal and patrilineal society?

Practice Essays

1. Compare and contrast the social organization of the Hopi and the Chinese.

2. How have women in rural Taiwan challenged certain stereotypes regarding their "powerless" status?

3. Who is the "kinkeeper" in your family? How does he or she maintain this role?

4. Describe the contemporary Chinese-Canadian kinship system. How does it differ from traditional systems of kinship among the Chinese?

5. Descent groups are convenient devices for solving a number of problems human societies commonly confront. Identify the problems and describe how a descent group solves them.

6. Discuss the forms and functions of descent groups.

7. Describe the work of anthropologist Charles Menzies and discuss the importance of anthropology with regards to the legal recognition of First Nations in Canada.

8. How do kinship terms reflect life in a society?

9. What is fictive kin? Are there any people in your life that can be considered "fictive kin"?

Solutions

Multiple-Choice Practice Questions

1. D
2. A
3. B
4. E
5. D
6. E
7. A
8. E
9. E
10. D
11. A
12. A
13. E
14. E
15. C
16. C
17. A
18. D
19. C
20. E
21. D
22. D
23. E
24. D
25. D
26. E
27. D
28. C
29. E
30. C
31. D

True/False Practice Questions

1. T
2. F
3. F
4. F
5. F
6. F
7. T
8. T
9. F
10. T
11. F
12. T
13. T
14. T
15. F
16. F
17. T
18. T

Chapter 9 ➤ *Kinship and Descent*

CHAPTER 10
SOCIAL STRATIFICATION AND GROUPINGS

SYNOPSIS

Challenge Issues: What principles, aside from kinship and marriage, do people use to organize societies? What are common-interest associations? What is social stratification? This chapter examines major kinds of non-kin organizations. Groups defined by gender, age, common interest, and class are described, as are various degrees of social mobility found in stratified societies. Stratified forms of social organization such as those involving class, ethnicity, or gender are presented near the conclusion of the chapter, as are the devastating effects of ethnic conflict.

CHAPTER OBJECTIVES

- grouping by gender
- age grouping
- common-interest associations
- social stratification
- anthropology applied: the Roma of Svinia
- gender perspectives: *Purdah*
- genocide in Rwanda

KEY TERMS

achieved status	functionalist theory of stratification	racism
age grade	gender stratification	social class
age set	institutionalized racism	social stratification
ascribed status	mobility	stratified societies
caste	open-class systems	symbolic indicators
closed-class systems	patterns of association	verbal evaluation
common-interest associations	power	wealth
conflict theory of stratification	prestige	
egalitarian cultures	race	

EXERCISES

Review Questions

1. Describe the value associated with aging among Yanomami women.

2. In what ways is age grouping evidenced in North America?

3. How does one become a member of an age grade?

118   *Chapter 10 ➤ Social Stratification and Groupings*

4. Distinguish between an age grade and an age set.

5. Describe the gender roles among the Huron of Southern Ontario.

6. How and why are common-interest associations formed?

7. Labels such as "teenagers" and "senior citizens" are examples of what?

8. Describe the gender groupings among the Mundurucu.

9. What purposes do urban-oriented associations serve?

10. How are elderly women viewed among the Yanomami?

11. Contrast an egalitarian society with a stratified society.

12. In what ways might a society be stratified?

13. Briefly describe India's caste system.

14. Describe some types of common-interest associations.

15. Define wealth, power and prestige.

Fill-in-the-Blank

1. An age_____is a category based on age, a stage through which people pass (such as a "teenager").
2. An age_____is a group of people who move through life stages together (such as "baby boomers").
3. Among the _____ of South America, men and women work, eat, and sleep separately.
4. Common-interest associations used to be called _____ associations.
5. The text suggests that the caste system is present not only in India but also in _____ and _____.
6. A_____ society is one in which members do not share equally in prestige and basic resources.
7. _____ is a special form of social class in which membership is determined by birth and remains fixed for life.
8. In a class society, people are theoretically able to change their class positions through social _____.
9. Societies that permit a great deal of social movement are described as _____ .
10. The *purdah* suggests that stratification based on _____ may be present.

Multiple-Choice Practice Questions

1. High rates of rape appear to be associated with societies in which the roles of males and females are highly segregated, and in which there are efforts by males to be dominant over women. If this is true, we would expect the highest rate of rape to occur among the _____ .
   a. Ju/'hoansi
   b. Mundurucu
   c. Iroquois
   d. Mbuti
   e. Hopi

2. In literate societies that rely on the written word for accumulated wisdom, elders are often _____ .
   a. treated with great respect because of their wisdom
   b. considered to be as valuable as their weight in gold
   c. treated like "living libraries" that contain much needed knowledge
   d. not considered sources of information
   e. killed when they turn sixty-five years old

3. The following _____are passed through by members of North American culture: toddler, teenager, senior citizen.
   a. age grades
   b. age sets
   c. social classes
   d. castes
   e. open classes

4. Which of the following statements about common-interest associations is *incorrect*?
    a. They were originally referred to in the anthropological literature as voluntary associations.
    b. Common-interest associations are more common in hunter-gatherer societies than in - urban-industrial societies.
    c. Common-interest associations are intimately associated with world urbanization and increasing social complexity.
    d. Common-interest associations are found in many traditional societies.
    e. Sometimes one can join a common-interest association voluntarily and sometimes membership is required by law.

5. A functionalist theory of stratification suggests that_____.
    a. equality is necessary for a society to function properly
    b. a power struggle takes place between the upper and lower levels of society
    c. inequality does not help a society function
    d. stratification is not a functional model of society
    e. inequality is necessary to maintain complex societies

6. Much of the inequality found in the world today is based on the concept of _____.
    a. age
    b. name
    c. race
    d. all of the above
    e. none of the above

7. A society composed of several groups that differ in their access to resources and prestige is said to be _____ .
    a. stratified
    b. unfair
    c. immoral
    d. egalitarian
    e. open

8. A/An_____ is a special form of social class in which membership is determined by birth and remains fixed for life.
    a. clan
    b. phratry
    c. common-interest association
    d. age group
    e. caste

Chapter 10 ➤ *Social Stratification and Groupings*   *121*

9. Symbolic indicators may not always be reliable in helping you assess someone's class status. Which of the following is an example of this?
    a. a common form of recreation of lower-class males is playing pool at the local beer joint
    b. a con man from a lower-class background wears a tuxedo when he tries to sell you shares in a nonexistent corporation
    c. according to Emily Post, one can always identify upper-crust families by the presence of a day maid
    d. Demille O'Hara, striving to return to the simplicity of life as lived by his tribal ancestors, lets his day maid go
    e. a con man from a lower-class background wears a tuxedo when he "tries to sell you shares in a nonexistent corporation," "Demille O'Hara, striving to return to the simplicity of life as lived by his tribal ancestors, lets his day maid go"

10. The ability to change one's class position is known as _____ .
    a. open class
    b. egalitarian
    c. social mobility
    d. indicative of common-interest societies
    e. inevitable

11. What is the major difference between Mundurucu and traditional European society?
    a. Women in Mundurucu society had some control over their economic activities, while European women did not.
    b. European women had some control over their economic activities, while Mundurucu women did not
    c. European men once believed that women ruled over men, but the roles reversed because women were unable to hunt.
    d. There are no major differences; women in both societies had very little control over their economic activities.
    e. none of the above

12. Which of the following *is not* a component of Franz Boas's rejection of the concept of race?
    a. A race is not an objective or demonstrable descent group.
    b. There is as much physical variation within a race as between races.
    c. One can make an assessment of mental strength based on physical characteristics.
    d. There are no clear-cut geographical and biological lines between the races.
    e. There is no correlation between race, on the one hand, and either mental or cultural characteristics on the other.

13. The concept of race _____ .
    a. first emerged in the 18th century
    b. was a way of justifying European colonial expansion and dominance
    c. is a culturally constructed concept, according to economic, political and social agendas, rather than a biological reality
    d. all of the above
    e. none of the above

14. A research project carried out by anthropologist_____ focused on the role of Filipina women working as domestic workers and nannies in Toronto and suggests that domestic work creates class, cultural, and racialized ethnic differences that are shaped by global economic forces.
    a. Geraldine Brooks
    b. David Sheffel
    c. Parin Dossa
    d. Charles Menzies
    e. Bonnie McElhinny

15. Anthropologist _____ stepped outside his role as an academic anthropologist and began to look for ways to improve the lives of the Roma after learning that the Roma of Svinia had a 100 percent unemployment rate, did not own any land, and were mostly illiterate.
    a. David Scheffel
    b. Charles Menzies
    c. Richard B. Lee
    d. P. R. Sanday
    e. none of the above

16. What the term_____ really refers to are those associations not based on sex, age, kinship, marriage, or territory that result from an act of joining.
    a. clan
    b. age grade
    c. voluntary association
    d. neighbourhood association
    e. women's auxiliary

17. Which of the following is not an example of a common-interest organization?
    a. Mothers Against Drunk Driving (MADD)
    b. the Kinsmen
    c. Canadian-Polish Congress
    d. Alcoholics Anonymous
    e. the Green Party

18. In what year was Africville, Nova Scotia, forcefully relocated?
    a. 1932
    b. 1951
    c. 1957
    d. 1962
    e. 1964

19. Which of the following is an example of institutionalized racism?
    a. the head tax for Chinese people in Canada, which rose from $50 in 1885 to $500 in 1903
    b. the denial of basic necessities, such as running water and electricity, for the residents of Africville
    c. the 1887 and 1907 anti-Chinese riots in Vancouver
    d. the vandalism of an Islamic school in Mississauga, Ontario on June 7, 2006
    e. all of the above

Chapter 10 ➤ *Social Stratification and Groupings*

20. Which of the following groups *has not* experienced some form of racism in Canada?
    a. Muslim Canadians
    b. Chinese immigrants
    c. First Nations peoples
    d. the people of Africville
    e. none of the above

21. Age grouping is so familiar and so important that it and _____ sometimes have been called the only universal factors for determining a person's position in society.
    a. height
    b. weight
    c. eye colour
    d. gender
    e. shoe size

22. The members of a/an _____ usually remain closely associated throughout their lives, or at least most of their lives.
    a. fraternity
    b. sorority
    c. union
    d. kindred
    e. age set

23. All stratified societies offer at least some _____, and this helps to ease the strains in any system of inequality.
    a. stability
    b. reliability
    c. instability
    d. mobility
    e. shakiness

24. In which of the following ways are societies stratified?
    a. gender
    b. age
    c. social class
    d. caste
    e. gender, age, social class, and caste

25. Dr. Scheffel's decision to step beyond his academic role and to engage actively in helping the Roma improve their way of life is an example of _____ anthropology.
    a. linguistic
    b. biological
    c. applied
    d. archaeological
    e. physical

26. Which of the following *is not* an example of a symbolic indicator of class?
    a. a brand new BMW
    b. the number of bathrooms in an individual's house
    c. occupation
    d. age
    e. a beat-up Honda

27. It is easily possible to distinguish between the Twa, Hutu, or Tutsi based on their _____.
    a. height
    b. knowledge of the person's ancestry
    c. culture
    d. religion
    e. none of the above

28. A caste-like system based on skin colour and wealth once existed in _____, where white minority created a political regime called apartheid.
    a. Germany
    b. Holland
    c. Belgium
    d. Sudan
    e. South Africa

True/False Practice Questions

1. Division of labour by sex is characteristic of all human societies.
   True or False

2. Usually an increase in the number of common-interest associations is associated with urbanization, but these associations are also found in traditional societies.
   True or False

3. Castes are strongly exogamous.
   True or False

4. Mobility refers to the ability to change one's class position.
   True or False

5. An age grade is a group of people initiated into the group at the same time who move though the series of categories together.
   True or False

6. "Baby boomers" are an example of an age set.
   True or False

7. In North America, people rely on the elderly for long-term memory and history.
   True or False

Chapter 10 ➤ *Social Stratification and Groupings*   *125*

8. The conflict theory of stratification suggests that inequality is necessary to maintain complex societies.
    True or False

9. Like age grades, age sets cease to exist after a specified number of years.
    True or False

10. Common-interest associations have proliferated in modern society, but are not found in many traditional societies.
    True or False

11. The Indian caste system has absolutely no flexibility and/or mobility.
    True or False

12. A caste-like system could never have existed in the United States.
    True or False

13. Individuals born and raised within large-scale societies face the challenge of succeeding within a complex social structure that extends well beyond kinship.
    True or False

Practice Short Answer Questions

1. To what degree does the Indian caste system allow for upward mobility? Explain your position.

2. What is an age set? Do you belong to an identifiable age set? Describe.

3. Under what conditions does social stratification become a problem?

4. What is grouping by age? Provide examples.

5. What is grouping by gender? Provide examples.

6. Distinguish between and describe the two perspectives on *purdah*, as discussed in your text.

7. Distinguish between class and caste.

8. What is institutionalized racism? Give two examples of institutionalized racism from your text.

9. What is social mobility and how does it function?

10. Who are the Roma of Svinia?

Practice Essays

1. Marx felt that religion was "the opiate of the masses," claiming that it was often used by the upper classes to perpetuate their own dominance. Can this perspective be applied to the Indian caste system? Would it be ethnocentric to do so?

2. Describe Canada's history of racial discrimination. Use examples from your text. Were there any accounts of racism that came as a surprise to you, or that you were unaware of?

3. Although important differences exist, there are nonetheless interesting similarities between Mundurucu beliefs and those of traditional European culture. Discuss those similarities.

4. Compare and contrast stratified societies with egalitarian cultures.

5. What role did colonialism play in the Rwandan genocide?

6. The classic ethnographic example of a caste system is the Hindu caste system of India. Describe that system.

7. Discuss the caste-like social system called apartheid that was established in South Africa.

8. Describe how social classes make life oppressive for large numbers of people, while at the same time performing an integrative function in society.

9. Discuss the relationship between immigration and discrimination in Canada.

SOLUTIONS

Fill-in-the-Blank

1. grade
2. set
3. Mundurucu
4. voluntary
5. South Africa and America
6. stratified
7. a caste
8. mobility
9. open-class systems
10. gender

Multiple-Choice Practice Questions

1.	B	**11.**	A	**21.**	D
2.	D	**12.**	C	**22.**	E
3.	A	**13.**	D	**23.**	D
4.	B	**14.**	E	**24.**	E
5.	E	**15.**	A	**25.**	C
6.	C	**16.**	C	**26.**	D
7.	A	**17.**	C	**27.**	B
8.	E	**18.**	E	**28.**	E
9.	E	**19.**	A		
10.	C	**20.**	E		

True/False Practice Questions

1.	T	**6.**	T	**11.**	F
2.	T	**7.**	F	**12.**	F
3.	F	**8.**	F	**13.**	T
4.	T	**9.**	F		
5.	F	**10.**	F		

CHAPTER 11
POLITICAL ORGANIZATION AND THE MAINTENANCE OF ORDER

SYNOPSIS

Challenge Issues: What is political organization? How is order maintained within a culture? How is order maintained between cultures? Are power and political organization different? How do political systems obtain people's allegiance? This chapter begins by exploring the four basic types of political systems as well as the role of women in Canadian politics. Social control, through the law, is also considered. Furthermore, the role of the role of the anthropologist as an aid in dispute resolution is investigated. Finally, political organization, political systems and the relationship between religion and politics is discussed.

CHAPTER OBJECTIVES

- kinds of political systems
- minority women in Canadian politics
- political organization and the maintenance of order
- limits on power in Bedouin society
- social control through law
- dispute resolution and the anthropologist
- political organization and external affairs
- political systems and the question of legitimacy
- religion and politics

KEY TERMS

adjudication	law	segmentary lineage system
band	mediation	social control
chiefdom	nation	state
consensus	naturalistic worldview	tribe
cultural control	negotiation	worldview
exploitative worldview	sanctions	

EXERCISES

Review Questions

1. What are the four basic kinds of political systems?

2. What kinds of societies typically have uncentralized systems?

3. How is authority conferred in a band?

4. How is authority conferred in a tribe?

5. What is the function of age-grade systems in the political structure of tribes?

6. Describe the role of the *tonowi* among the Kapauku Papuans.

7. What kinds of societies typically have centralized political systems?

8. Distinguish between nation and state.

9. What has women's role generally been in political leadership?

10. Describe women's role in Igbo society.

11. How is social control generally maintained in bands and tribes?

12. How do internalized controls guide behaviour?

13. Distinguish between positive and negative sanctions.

14. Distinguish between informal and formal sanctions.

15. Why is the definition of law destined to be inexact?

16. What are the functions of law?

17. Differentiate between negotiation, adjudication, and mediation.

18. How are disputes handled by the Kpelle?

19. Why might warfare be so prominent in food-producing societies?

20. How is the Abenaki worldview reflected in their hunting practices?

21. In what ways is religion connected with politics?

Fill-in-the-Blank

1. The term _____ refers to the system of social relationships that is connected with the maintenance of public order.
2. The attitudes of the Abenaki hunters tend to exemplify a _____ worldview.
3. Anthropologists have identified four types of political systems; two are said to be _____ and two are _____ .
4. An egalitarian, autonomous small group composed of related people who occupy a single region is called a _____ .
5. All humans were foragers living in band-type organizations until about_____ years ago.
6. The _____ are an example of a society practicing band-level organization.
7. Most conflict in bands is settled by informal means, and decisions are usually made by _____ .
8. A _____ is a larger grouping than a band and is linked to a specific territory.
9. The Kpelle are ruled by a _____ .
10. The smallest unit of the Swazi government was the _____ .
11. In tribal societies of Melanesia, a type of leader called the _____ or *tonowi* is prevalent.
12. A _____ is a ranked society in which every member has a position in the hierarchy.
13. Chiefdoms are linked to _____ economic systems.
14. The Swazi have a _____ -level political system.
15. States are typically linked to _____ subsistence patterns.
16. An example of a society in which women play a notably strong political role is the _____ .
17. The Wape of New Guinea use belief in _____ as a means of social control.
18. In North America we rely on both external and _____ controls to maintain social order.
19. The Inuit use _____ as a means of resolving conflict.

20. Western societies make a distinction between _____ law, involving offences committed against individuals, and _____ law, involving offences committed against the state.

21. Disputes may be settled by _____ , the use of direct argument and compromise by the disputing parties, or by _____ , settlement through the assistance of an unbiased third party.

22. Warfare is most closely linked to the _____ -type political system.

Multiple-Choice Practice Questions

1. A small group of related households occupying a particular region that gather periodically but that do not yield their sovereignty to the larger collective can be described as a _____.
   a. tribe
   b. band
   c. *kxau*
   d. council
   e. government

2. Both bands and tribes tend to be _____ .
   a. centralized
   b. associated with industrialism
   c. dependent on age groups for political organization
   d. uncentralized and unstratified
   e. hierarchical in social organization

3. The form of social organization typical of hunter-gatherers is the _____ , whereas horticulture and pastoralism are usually associated with the form of social organization called the

   _____ .
   a. tribe/chiefdom
   b. tribe/state
   c. tribe/band
   d. band/chiefdom
   e. band/tribe

4. Together with Roger Fisher, _____ authored what has come to be known as the negotiator's "bible": *Getting to Yes: Negotiating Agreement without Giving In.*
   a.   William L. Ury
   b.   Bronislaw Malinowski
   c.   E. Adamson Hoebel
   d.   Bernard Saladin d'Anglure
   e.   none of the above

5. In the Igbo system, the women _____ .
   a. managed their own affairs
   b. had their interests represented at all levels of government
   c. had the right to enforce their decisions and rules with sanctions similar to those employed by men.
   d. all of the above
   e. none of the above

6. A _____ is a ranked society in which every member has a position in the hierarchy and an individual's status is determined by membership in a descent group.
   a. band
   b. tribe
   c. chiefdom
   d. state
   e. kindred

7. The state is distinctive in the extensiveness of its legitimate use of _____ to regulate the affairs of its citizens.
   a. kinship
   b. force
   c. chiefs
   d. religion
   e. gossip

8. In a chiefdom, an individual's status is determined by membership in a _____ .
   a. government
   b. social class
   c. bureaucracy
   d. descent group
   e. secret society

9. The Wape concern about ancestral ghosts is a good example of _____ control.
   a. externalized
   b. social
   c. internalized or cultural
   d. formal sanctions
   e. negative sanctions

10. At the heart of political organization is _____ .
    a. control of unacceptable social behaviour
    b. the legitimate use of force to maintain order
    c. unequal access to power
    d. the dominance of males over females
    e. the development of egalitarian relationships

Chapter 11 ➤ *Political Organization and the Maintenance of Social Order*   *133*

11. Sanctions refer to _____ .
    a. internalized social controls
    b. holy behaviour
    c. externalized social controls
    d. decadent behaviour
    e. ritualized behaviour

12. _____ sanctions attempt to precisely and explicitly regulate people's behaviour. They can be positive (such as military decorations) or negative (such as imprisonment).
    a. hierarchical
    b. egalitarian
    c. informal
    d. formal
    e. magical

13. Which of the following *is not* involved in gaining and maintaining respect among the Bedouin?
    a. adhering to the ideals of honour
    b. provide for and protect their dependents
    c. be fair
    d. asserting authority forcefully
    e. take no undue advantage of their position

14. The functions of law include_____ .
    a. the definition of proper behaviour in particular circumstances so that everyone is clear about their rights and duties
    b. protecting the wealthy from the poor
    c. redefining what is proper behaviour when situations change
    d. allocating authority to use coercion to enforce sanctions
    e. "the definition of proper behaviour in particular circumstances so that everyone is clear about their rights and duties," "redefining what is proper behaviour when situations change," and "allocating authority to use coercion to enforce sanctions"

15. A method of resolving disputes in which the disputing parties voluntarily arrive at a mutually satisfactory agreement is called _____ .
    a. negotiation
    b. mediation
    c. adjudication
    d. use of sanctions
    e. law

16. Which of the following are likely to be associated with warfare?
    a. centralized political systems
    b. the rise of cities
    c. a technology that supports population growth
    d. possession of complex, valuable property
    e. all of the above

17. An exploitative world view is more likely to exist in which of the following technologies?
    a. foraging
    b. horticulture
    c. pastoralism
    d. intensive agriculture
    e. horticulture, pastoralism, and intensive agriculture

18. Disputes among the Nuer are frequent; however, the possible source of social disruption is minimized by the actions of the _____.
    a. king
    b. official chief
    c. shaman
    d. leopard-skin chief
    e. headman

19. The *obi* and *omu* were part of _____ society.
    a. Kapauku
    b. Navajo
    c. Algonquian
    d. Aztec
    e. Igbo

20. Another agent of control in societies, whether or not they possess centralized political systems, may be _____.
    a. witchcraft
    b. sorcerers
    c. ostracism
    d. fines set by judges
    e. warriors

21. An important pioneer in the anthropological study of law was _____ .
    a. Eleanor Leacock
    b. Jody Williams
    c. John Wesley Powell
    d. E. Adamson Hoebel
    e. Bernard Saladin d'Anglure

22. The field of _____ is one of growing anthropological involvement and employment.
    a. ethnoscience
    b. ethnology
    c. dispute control
    d. dispute resolution
    e. assertiveness training

Chapter 11 ➤ *Political Organization and the Maintenance of Social Order*

23. _____founded the Association Inuksiutiit Katimajit, the primary purpose of which was to return his research data to the Inuit. They also established the *International Journal of Inuit Studies (Études Inuit)*.
    a. Sue Ellen Jacobs
    b. William L. Ury
    c. Bernard Saladin d'Anglure
    d. Roger Fisher
    e. Herald Prins

24. When one refers to the way power is distributed and embedded in society, one is referring to a society's _____.
    a. social organization
    b. military structure
    c. political ideology
    d. class structure
    e. political organization

25. The ability to control others' behaviour, whether organizing a seal hunt or raising a military force, has to do with the way power is distributed and embedded in a society, or its _____.
    a. political organization
    b. social class structure
    c. political ideology
    d. police force
    e. social system

26. Nation-states with centralized governments make a clear distinction between offences against the state and offences against individuals, usually termed under the headings of criminal versus _____ offences.
    a. private
    b. individual
    c. personal
    d. civil
    e. municipal

27. It is clear that war is not a universal phenomenon, for in various parts of the world there are societies that do not practice warfare as we know it. Which of the following groups of people is *not* an example of a group that does not practice warfare?
    a. the Ju/'hoansi of southern Africa
    b. the Arapesh of New Guinea
    c. the Hopi of the American southwest
    d. all of the above practice warfare
    e. none of the above practice warfare

28. Scholars have identified four basic kinds of political systems and categorized them into uncentralized and centralized. Which of the following would be considered uncentralized systems?
    a. chiefdoms
    b. tribes
    c. states
    d. bands
    e. tribes and bands

29. Two models have been presented to analyze inequality within the Canadian political system: _____ and _____ .
    a. similarity/compensation
    b. similarity/component
    c. component/shared
    d. shared/compensation
    e. compensation/component

30. In order to escape an unhappy marriage, Náfla, a Bedouin woman, pretended _____.
    a. to be unable to bear children
    b. she had been sexually active prior to marriage
    c. to be possessed
    d. to be very ill
    e. none of the above

31. _____ systems provide a tribal society with a means of political integration beyond the kin group.
    a. Age-grade
    b. Common-interest association
    c. Segmentary lineage
    d. Kindred
    e. Clan

32. Although leaders of chiefdoms are almost always men, in some cultures a politically astute wife, sister, or single daughter of a deceased male chief could inherit that position. One historical example is Queen _____, who succeeded her half brother as leader of the Polynesian chiefdom of Tahiti in 1827.
    a. Liliokalnai
    b. Latifah
    c. Wilhelmina
    d. Pomare IV
    e. Isabella

33. _____ equals legitimacy when the ideas of the ruling class are identified not as the narrow interests of the dominant elite, but rather as expressing the "natural" order of things and simple "common sense."
    a. ideology
    b. government
    c. power
    d. hegemony
    e. control

Chapter 11 ➤ *Political Organization and the Maintenance of Social Order*

True/False Practice Questions

1. Negative sanctions are called laws if they are formalized.
   True or False

2. Until recently, many non-Western peoples had no fixed form of government in the sense that Westerners understand the term.
   True or False

3. The Ju/'hoansi have a tribal-type political organization.
   True or False

4. The Big Man of the Kapauku is called *tonowi*.
   True or False

5. Chiefdoms and states both have luxury goods available for certain groups of people.
   True or False

6. In many tribal societies the organizing unit is the clan.
   True or False

7. The *tonowi* acquires political power through his loans.
   True or False

8. The Arapesh of New Guinea are known to practice warfare.
   True or False

9. A form of settlement that involves a third party is called mediation.
   True or False

10. In 1957, Prime Minister Lester B. Pearson received the Nobel Peace Prize for his establishment of an international peacekeeping force within the United Nations Security Council.
    True or False

11. The greater vulnerability of the poor to disease is a prime example of structural violence.
    True or False

12. The necessity of "the war on terror" and the inevitability of the market are examples of natural, common sense concepts.
    True or False

13. The term political organization refers to the way power is distributed and embedded in society.
    True or False

14. It is clear that war is a universal phenomenon.
    True or False

15. Among foragers, with their uncentralized political systems, warfare is all but unknown.
    True or False

16. Among the Igbo of Midwestern Nigeria, women were not allowed positions in the administrative hierarchy.
True or False

17. Western societies do not clearly distinguish offences against the state from offences against individuals.
True or False

Practice Matching

Match each culture to its description.

1. _____ Azande
2. _____ Swazi
3. _____ Igbo
4. _____ Wape
5. _____ Abenaki

a. Nigerian society in which men and women occupy separate political spheres
b. foragers in the historic past that lived in harmony with their environment, exemplifying a naturalistic worldview
c. a southeast African nation
d. a New Guinea people in the historical past with effective informal and internalized controls
e. a group in the Sudan that practices witchcraft

Short Answer

1. Why is it incorrect to blame political unrest in many parts of the world on "tribalism"?

2. Identify the countries where women have recently been elected and served as presidents or prime ministers.

3. Describe the ways in which force can be resisted by women among the Bedouin. Consider Náfla's story.

4. Distinguish between and describe the two models presented to analyze inequality toward women within the Canadian political system.

5. Explain formal and informal sanctions.

6. What is witchcraft and how does it contribute to social control of human societies?

7. What is the evolution of warfare?

8. What is legitimacy and how does it affect authority and power?

9. Compare and contrast the tribe and band as institutions of political organization.

Chapter 11 ➤ *Political Organization and the Maintenance of Social Order*

Practice Essays

1. Why has the state-type system expanded to encompass most of the globe today? Explore how band, tribe, and chiefdom organizations might persist within a world order based primarily on states.

2. What are the limits on Bedouin power? Are they similar to the types of limits we place on power in Canada?

3. Who is William L. Ury? What is his area of expertise? What is he trying to accomplish?

4. Who is Bernard Saladin d'Anglure? What is his impact on anthropology? What type of responsibility do anthropologists have to the people they study?

5. What is "hegemony"? Give several examples of hegemony in Canada and describe the ways in which they exemplify the concept of hegemony.

6. The case of Wolf Lies Down and the Elk Soldier Society, from Hoebel's *The Law of Primitive Man* (1954) clearly illustrates three basic functions of law. Describe these functions.

7. Would you describe Canada's worldview as exploitative or naturalistic? Expand upon and justify your response.

8. Historically, what has been Canada's role in international peacekeeping?

9. What role do women play within the political system among the Igbo of Nigeria? Compare this to the role of women in the Canadian political sphere.

SOLUTIONS

Fill-in-the-Blank

1. political organization
2. naturalistic
3. uncentralized, centralized
4. band
5. 10,000
6. Ju/'hoansi
7. consensus
8. tribe
9. paramount chief
10. homestead
11. Big Man
12. chiefdom
13. redistributive
14. state
15. intensive
16. Iroquois
17. ghosts
18. internal

19. song duels
20. criminal, civil
21. negotiation, mediation
22. state

Multiple-Choice Practice Questions

1.	B	12.	D	23.	B
2.	D	13.	D	24.	E
3.	E	14.	E	25.	A
4.	A	15.	A	26.	E
5.	D	16	E	27.	E
6.	C	17.	E	28.	E
7.	B	18.	D	29.	A
8.	D	19.	E	30.	C
9.	C	20.	A	31.	A
10.	A	21.	D	32.	D
11.	C	22.	D	33.	D

True/False Practice Questions

1.	T	7.	T	13.	T
2.	T	8.	F	14.	F
3.	F	9.	T	15.	T
4.	T	10.	T	16.	F
5.	T	11.	T	17.	F
6.	T	12.	F		

Practice Matching

1. E
2. C
3. A
4. D
5. B

CHAPTER 12
RELIGION AND THE SUPERNATURAL

SYNOPSIS

Challenge Issues: What is religion? What are identifying features of religion? Why is religion a cultural universal? This chapter discusses the universality of religion, considering the functions served by religious belief and ritual in the social order. The authors compare various kinds of supernatural beings and the relationships among witchcraft, magic, and religion. The role of religion in culture change is also explored.

CHAPTER OBJECTIVES

- the anthropological approach to religion
- the practice of religion
- understanding Islam
- menstrual taboo
- religion, magic, and witchcraft
- aboriginal men and traditional healing in Canadian prisons
- neo-pagan religions
- roles of religion
- religion and culture change

KEY TERMS

animatism	pantheon	separation
animism	polytheism	shaman/medicine person
cargo cults	priest or priestess	taboo
contagious magic	reconstructionist religions	transition
imitative magic	religion	wicca
incorporation	revitalization movements	witchcraft
myth	rites of intensification	
neo-paganism	rites of passage	

EXERCISES

Review Questions

1. Why has there been a recent turn toward religious fundamentalism?

2. What are the "Five Pillars of Islam"?

3. What are the three major groupings of supernatural beings?

4. What is the role of gods and goddesses in many societies?

5. Describe the role of the "trickster" in Ju/'hoansi mythology.

6. Which four themes characterize the Islamic revivalism movement?

7. What purpose do ancestral spirits serve?

8. In what type of society is one likely to find animism?

9. Distinguish between animism and animatism.

10. In what type of society is one likely to find priestesses?

11. How are shamans made and how do they carry out their work?

12. What benefits do people derive from enlisting the services of a shaman?

13. What are two main types of ritual?

14. What are the three stages in a rite of passage, according to Van Gennep?

15. What is the "menstrual taboo"?

16. Why are rites of intensification performed?

17. Distinguish between the two fundamental principles of magic.

18. Describe the distinction between "black witches" and "white witches" among the Ibibio.

19. What are the psychological functions of religion?

20. What are the social functions of religion?

Chapter 12 ➤ *Religion and the Supernatural*

Fill-in-the-Blank

1. A hallmark of religion is belief in _____ .
2. In the nineteenth century, European thinkers believed that _____ would eventually eclipse religion.
3. The set of gods and goddesses in a society are called its _____ .
4. In most societies with subsistence bases in _____ or _____ , deities are conceptualized as masculine.
5. A belief that nature is animated by spirits is called _____ .
6. A concept of impersonal power, such as mana, is called _____ .
7. _____ are specialists who have acquired spiritual power, which they can use on behalf of human clients.
8. _____ was a pioneer in the study of rites of passage.
9. When Mende girls are initiated into adult society, they undergo _____ .
10. A ceremony to bring rain to a drought-stricken community is a _____ .
11. The three stages of a life crisis ritual are _____ , _____ , and _____ .
12. _____ wrote *The Golden Bough*.
13. _____ magic is based on the assumption that things that are similar to each other have an effect on each other.
14. Assuming that a person's fingernail clippings, hair, blood, and so on retain a spiritual connection to that person is the basis for _____ magic.
15. Among the Ibibio, _____ beliefs are highly developed and long-standing.
16. Founded by Gerald Gardner in 1951, _____ is a modern version of an ancient magical religion.

Multiple-Choice Practice Questions

1. Baltic, Celtic, Druidism, Hellenismos and Kemetism are examples of _____ religions.
   a. revivalism
   b. rebuilding
   c. revitalization
   d. reconstructionist
   e. wiccan

2. _____ may be defined as the beliefs and patterns of behaviour by which people try to control those aspects of the universe that are otherwise beyond their control.
   a. political organization
   b. government
   c. kinship
   d. common-interest associations
   e. religion

144 *Chapter 12 ➤ Religion and the Supernatural*

3. Which one of the following options best describes Millenarian cults?
   a. They are responses to profound, rapid social change.
   b. They help deal with the stress arising when traditional beliefs fail to explain life-altering Upheavals.
   c. They tend to follow a specific pattern.
   d. all of the above
   e. none of the above

4. A people's collection of gods and goddesses is called a _____.
   a. mana
   b. shaman
   c. pantheon
   d. priest
   e. fetish

5. Belief in a supreme being who controls the universe is usually associated with _____.
   a. bands
   b. tribes
   c. chiefdoms
   d. states
   e. multinational corporations

6. If religious belief reflects the structure of society, in which types of society would you expect to find widespread belief in ancestral spirits?
   a. those in which descent groups play a major role in social organization
   b. those with a disproportionately large number of old people
   c. those with a disproportionately large number of young people
   d. those in which neolocal marital residence are the rule
   e. those with egocentric systems such as the kindred

7. The belief that nature is animated with spirits is called _____.
   a. animation
   b. anima
   c. animatism
   d. animism
   e. ennui

8. A _____ is a full-time religious specialist who occupies an office that has a certain rank and function.
   a. shaman
   b. priest/priestess
   c. witch
   d. magician
   e. diviner

Chapter 12 ➤ Religion and the Supernatural   145

9. In acting as a healer, the shaman _____ .
   a. accurately diagnoses medical problems
   b. may improve the patient's state of mind, which aids in recovery
   c. may be coping with his or her own problems by becoming intensely involved with the problems of others
   d. provides reassurance to the community through an elaborate drama that may involve trickery
   e. "may improve the patient's state of mind, which aids in recovery," "may be coping with his or her own problems by becoming intensely involved with the problems of others," and "provides reassurance to the community through an elaborate drama that may involve trickery"

10. Ceremonies such as bar mitzvah, elaborate weddings, baby showers, and graduation parties that help individuals make major changes in their lives are referred to as rites of _____ .
    a. transition
    b. intensification
    c. separation
    d. passage
    e. incorporation

11. The _____ taboo has been referenced by feminists and some anthropologists to support the notion of universal male dominance and oppression of women.
    a. circumcision
    b. isolation
    c. menstruation
    d. scarification
    e. witchcraft

12. In *The Golden Bough*, _____ distinguished between religion and magic.
    a. Bronislaw Malinowski
    b. Franz Boas
    c. Sir James Frazer
    d. Sir Edward Tylor
    e. Clifford Geertz

13. Many magical incantations require the use of fingernail clippings of the intended victim. This is an example of _____ .
    a. imitative magic
    b. contagious magic
    c. witch magic
    d. nightmare magic
    e. scientific thinking

14. Magic involves the manipulation of powers for good or evil, whereas witchcraft involves the possession of an innate power used for _____ .
    a. religious purposes
    b. scientific reasons
    c. malevolent or benevolent purposes
    d. traditional societies
    e. societies that lack religion

15. Religion, magic, and witchcraft are all *similar* in which of the following ways?
    a. They all disappear once modern education and scientific training expand.
    b. They all share the common goal of improving social relationships within a community.
    c. They are all associated with morose nonconformists who try to destroy society.
    d. They provide explanations of events and are mechanisms of social control.
    e. They are all morally neutral.

16. A belief in _____ enables people to explain why things go wrong by blaming certain individuals who are said to have the internal psychic ability to cause harm to others.
    a. witchcraft
    b. magic
    c. divination
    d. contagion
    e. evil

17. Which of the following illustrate the psychological functions of religion?
    a. Among the Holy Ghost People of the United States, handling snakes and drinking strychnine is a common feature of their worship; one explanation of this behaviour is that by confronting the possibility of death, they achieve a sense of awe and transcendence.
    b. An Islamic judge who orders the hand of a thief cut off can sleep soundly at night because he thinks of himself as merely the agent of divinely inspired justice.
    c. The Navajo Indian origin myth provides every Navajo with a sense of this place in an orderly Universe.
    d. A person raised in the Catholic religion feels tremendous guilt when she/he commits a wrong.
    e. "Among the Holy Ghost People of the United States, handling snakes and drinking strychnine is a common feature of their worship; one explanation of this behaviour is that by confronting the possibility of death, they achieve a sense of awe and transcendence"; "an Islamic judge who orders the hand of a thief cut off can sleep soundly at night because he thinks of himself as merely the agent of divinely inspired justice"; and "the Navajo Indian origin myth provides every Navajo with a sense of this place in an orderly universe."

18. A _____ is a deliberate effort by members of a society to construct a more satisfying culture.
    a. divination
    b. rite of intensification
    c. fetish
    d. lineage system
    e. revitalization movement

19. Which of the following statements about revitalization movements is *incorrect*?
    a. The purpose of revitalization movements is to reform society.
    b. Revitalization movements always fail because they require too much change to be tolerated.
    c. All known major religions, including Judaism, Christianity, and Islam, began as revitalization movements.
    d. Revitalization movements may be completely unrealistic.
    e. Revitalization movements may be adaptive and give rise to long-lasting religions.

Chapter 12 ➤ *Religion and the Supernatural*

20. There are _____ versions of the Iroquois origin myth.
    a. about 10
    b. 13
    c. 27
    d. 32
    e. over 40

21. Anthropologists no longer make a distinction between _____ and _____.
    a. religion/witchcraft
    b. witchcraft/the supernatural
    c. religion/magic
    d. magic/witchcraft
    e. the supernatural/magic

22. Which of the following is not one of the four basic statements of the Qur'an?
    a. A person is absolutely subject to the will of Allah in all matters.
    b. A person must carry out the tasks which Allah assigns to her/him.
    c. Allah created the world.
    d. After this life, Allah will reward or punish each person in the measure in which he/she has lived according to the will of Allah.
    e. Each Muslim must make a pilgrimage to Mecca at least once in his/her lifetime.

23. The _____ are careful to conceal their extracted teeth, because these might fall into the hands of certain mythical beings that could harm the owners of the teeth by working mahoc on them.
    a. Trobrianders
    b. Wiccan
    c. Ju/'hoansi
    d. Basutos
    e. Ibibio

24. Religion is viewed most simply as organized belief in the _____ , and every religion fulfills numerous social and psychological needs.
    a. Christianity
    b. social system
    c. supernatural
    d. prevailing culture
    e. magic

25. _____ is a neo-pagan religion involving elements of polytheism and animism.
    a. Wicca
    b. Reform Judaism
    c. New Catholicism
    d. Seventh Day Adventist
    e. Atheism

148   Chapter 12 ➤ Religion and the Supernatural

26. Faith healers and many other evangelists among fundamentalist Christians share most of the characteristics of _____.
    a. Buddhism
    b. Shintoism
    c. Taoism
    d. shamanism
    e. socialism

27. In Salem, Massachusetts, _____ suspected witches were arrested in 1692.
    a. 50
    b. 100
    c. 200
    d. 2000
    e. 2050

28. Usually myths portray supernatural beings in ways that illustrate the culture's _____ code in action.
    a. spiritual
    b. ethical
    c. belief
    d. supernatural
    e. relationship

29. Anthropologist _____ defined religion as "a set of rituals, rationalized by myth, which mobilizes supernatural powers for the purpose of achieving or preventing transformations of state in man and nature."
    a. E. E. Evans-Pritchard
    b. E. Adamson Hoebel
    c. Hilda Kuper
    d. A. R. Radcliffe-Brown
    e. Anthony F. C. Wallace

30. The _____trickster is portrayed in myths as tricking and punishing youths who mock others, lie, are greedy, or go in for extremes of behaviour.
    a. Blackfoot
    b. Celtic
    c. Nordic
    d. Aztec
    e. Mayan

31. This Canadian anthropologist's understanding of Dene-zaa myths, dreams, and visions has provided extraordinary insight into their thought world.
    a. Richard B. Lee
    b. Jillian Ridington
    c. Robin Ridington
    d. Anthony F.C. Wallace
    e. Colin Turnbull

Chapter 12 ➤ Religion and the Supernatural

32. The rites of passage that help individuals through the crucial crises of their lives can be divided into three stages. Which of the following would be those stages?
    a. separation
    b. transition
    c. incorporation
    d. acquisition
    e. separation, transition, and incorporation

33. _____ forms part of a cultural system's superstructure, which comprises a society's worldview.
    a. political philosophy
    b. economic organization
    c. social structure
    d. religion
    e. the arts

True/False Practice Questions

1. The belief that nature is animated by spirits is called animism.
   True or False

2. Among foragers, religion tends to be separated from daily life and activity.
   True or False

3. Rites of intensification help individuals get through a crisis.
   True or False

4. Religion provides an orderly model of the universe and reduces fear and anxiety.
   True or False

5. Gods and goddesses are the most powerful and remote of supernatural beings.
   True or False

6. Ancestral spirits are mostly always malevolent.
   True or False

7. Roger Ridington failed to incorporate a collaborative approach to ethnography.
   True or False

8. To the Doukhobors, God is not a supernatural being.
   True or False

9. The Judaic and Christian account of creation in the Bible's book of Genesis is an example of myth in a literate culture.
   True or False

10. Religious activity may be less prominent in the lives of social elites.
    True or False

11. Religion is viewed most simply as organized belief in the supernatural that does not fulfill any social and psychological needs.
True or False

12. Science, with its creation of new technologies, has helped diminish religious practice worldwide.
True or False

13. Menstrual taboos are only present in a few cultures.
True or False

14. Aboriginal healing programs have proven effective in preventing recidivism, according to recent studies.
True or False

15. Far from causing the death of religion, the growth of scientific knowledge, by producing new anxieties and raising new questions about human existence, may have contributed to the continuing practice of religion in modern life.
True or False

Practice Matching

Match the culture/religion with its characteristic.

1. _____ Wiccan
2. _____ Druids
3. _____ Ibibio
4. _____ Sioux
5. _____ Mende

a. West African people who practice female initiation rite involving female circumcision
b. Southwestern Native Americans with a witchcraft tradition
c. embrace a belief system evolving polytheism and animism
d. a polytheistic group who follow a calendar based on stages of the sun, earth and moon
e. Sub-Saharan African people with a witchcraft tradition

Short Answer

1. Discuss the relationship between worldview and religion.

2. What is contagious magic? Provide examples.

3. What is the anthropological definition of the term "shaman"?

4. What are rites of intensification? Provide examples.

5. What are rites of passage? Explain each of the stages.

6. Compare and contrast priests and shamans.

7. What is magic? Provide examples.

Chapter 12 ➤ *Religion and the Supernatural*

8. What are revitalization movements? How do they contribute to society?

9. Define witchcraft.

10. What are ancestral spirits?

11. What is fundamentalism? Provide examples from the text.

Practice Essays

1. Bronislaw Malinowski, in his classic essay "Magic, Science, and Religion," claimed that each of these was a viable mode of cognition and that most societies exhibit all of them in variable proportions. In what ways does magical thinking persist in contemporary North America? Is it likely to persist into the future?

2. Fundamentalism is an often misunderstood concept. Describe and discuss some of the misconceptions regarding fundamentalist movements.

3. Describe the process of incorporating aboriginal healing practices in Canadian prisons. Do you believe these programs should be part of the Canadian prison system? Consider the evidence from the text.

4. What is shamanism and how can the widespread occurrence of shamanism be explained?

5. Religious rituals are religion in action. Describe what in fact is accomplished by religious rituals.

6. What is a revitalization movement? Explain how and why do they come into existence.

7. Describe Islamic revivalism. What reasons are given for this revival?

8. What are some of the shared assumptions of anthropologists in their approach to the study of religion? What are some of the challenges faced by anthropologists when trying to define "religion"?

9. If you practice a religion, describe your own religion. Are there associated myths and/or beliefs? How is your religion evidenced in your daily activities? If you do not practice a religion, describe your personal belief system and how it is manifested in your daily life.

SOLUTIONS

Fill-in-the-Blank

1. supernatural beings
2. science
3. pantheon
4. animal herding, intensive agriculture
5. animism
6. animatism
7. Shamans
8. Arnold Van Gennep
9. female circumcision
10. rite of intensification
11. separation, transition, incorporation
12. Sir James George Frazer
13. imitative
14. contagious
15. witchcraft
16. wicca

Multiple-Choice Practice Questions

1. D	**12.** C	**23.** D
2. E	**13.** B	**24.** C
3. E	**14.** C	**25.** A
4. D	**15.** D	**26.** D
5. D	**16.** A	**27.** C
6. A	**17.** E	**28.** B
7. D	**18.** E	**29.** E
8. B	**19.** B	**30.** A
9. E	**20.** E	**31.** C
10. D	**21.** C	**32.** E
11. C	**22.** E	**33.** D

True/False Practice Questions

1. T	**6.** F	**11.** F
2. F	**7.** T	**12.** F
3. F	**8.** T	**13.** F
4. T	**9.** T	**14.** F
5. T	**10.** F	**15.** T

Practice Matching

1. B	**3.** E	**5.** A
2. D	**4.** C	

CHAPTER 13
THE ARTS

SYNOPSIS

Challenge Issues: What is art? Why do anthropologists study art? What are the functions of art? This chapter examines the ethnocentric assumptions implicit in most Western definitions of the arts and artists. It distinguishes different types of creative activity, such as the visual and verbal arts, music and body arts and attempts to come up with a cross-culturally valid definition of art. The chapter concludes with a discussion of artistic censorship.

CHAPTER OBJECTIVES

- the anthropological study of art
- verbal art
- protecting cultural heritages
- the mock wedding: folk drama in the prairie provinces
- the art of music
- visual art
- on being a man
- body art
- censorship

KEY TERMS

ethnomusicology	folkloristics	motif
folklore	legends	tale

EXERCISES

Review Questions

1. Distinguish between secular and religious art.

2. What are the basic kinds of verbal arts studied by anthropologists?

3. Give an example of how myth expresses the world view of a people.

4. Distinguish between legend and myth.

5. Who is Julie Cruikshank and what were her contributions to anthropology?

154   *Chapter 13 ➤ The Arts*

6. What role does poetry play in the lives of the Bedouins?

7. What type of society is likely to have epics? Why?

8. What aspects of legends are of interest to anthropologists?

9. Why are anthropologists interested in tales?

10. What are the functions of music?

11. What is body painting? Describe some examples of body painting from the text.

12. Briefly recount the history of tattooing.

13. What is folkloristics?

14. What is ethnomusicology?

15. Describe three pieces of Canadian visual art.

Fill-in-the-Blank

1. The term "verbal arts" is preferred to the term _____ , a term developed in the nineteenth century to refer to traditional oral stories of European peasants.
2. The word "myth," in_____usage, refers to something that is widely believed to be true but is not.
3. Tabaldak and Odziozo are characters in the origin myth of the _____.
4. Legends are _____narratives that recount the deeds of heroes, the movements of people, and the establishment of customs.
5. A surprising number of motifs in European and African folktales are traceable to ancient sources in _____ .
6. "Little songs" that occur every day were studied among the _____ .
7. The study of music in its cultural setting is called _____ .
8. In Australia, traditional aboriginal _____ have taken on a legal function, as they are being introduced into court as evidence of early settlement patterns.
9. _____ is an art form that has become the voice of disaffected youth; however, it is often viewed as vandalism.

Chapter 13 ➤ _The Arts_

10. Two people playing different patterns of beats at the same time is called _____ .

11. In some First Nations artwork on Canada's northwest coast, animal figures may be so highly _____ as to be difficult for an outsider to recognize.

12. _____'s powerful watercolours and field sketches have provided a valuable record of western Canadian life in the mid-1800s.

13. The most universal site for piercing is the_____.

Multiple-Choice Practice Questions

1. Whether useful or non-useful, all art is an expression of _____ .
   a. the innate need to be impractical
   b. a fundamental human capacity for religious expression
   c. state-level societies that can afford specialists
   d. political domination of minorities by elites
   e. the symbolic representation of form and the expression of feeling that constitutes creativity

2. The observation that all cultures include activities that provide aesthetic pleasure suggests that _____ .
   a. humans may have an innate or acquired need to produce art
   b. the human mind requires the stimulation of imaginative play to prevent boredom
   c. all societies, from food-foraging bands to industrial states, include art in their culture
   d. art is a necessary activity in which all normal, active members of society participate
   e. all of the above

3. Anthropologists prefer to use the term *verbal arts* rather than the term *folklore* because the term _____.
   a. folklore is used only by linguists; the term verbal arts is used only by anthropologists
   b. verbal arts sounds more sophisticated
   c. verbal arts is more scientific
   d. folklore implies lack of sophistication and is a condescending term to use
   e. folklore refers only to fairy tales

4. The type of verbal arts that has received the most study and attention is _____.
   a. poetry
   b. incantations
   c. narratives
   d. proverbs
   e. riddles

5. In the myth of Tabaldak and Odziozo, Tabaldak first created the Abenakis from stone and then from living wood. What does this tell us about the functions of myth?
   a. Myths function to tell actual history; the Abenakis believe that they were originally made of wood.
   b. Myths bring humour into the lives of the Abenakis because the myths are so ridiculous.
   c. Myths function primarily to provide entertainment; the Abenakis know they were not made from wood, but like to tell this story to visiting anthropologists who are so gullible.
   d. Myths function to express a culture's world view; the Abenakis see themselves as belonging to the world of living things rather than to the non-living world of stone.
   e. Myths provide skills of woodworking and stone masonry to the Abenakis.

6. Because legends contain details of a people's past, they are a form of history; because they often give a picture of a people's view of the world and humanity's place in it, they are like

   _____ .
   a. poetry
   b. religion
   c. magic
   d. kinship systems
   e. myths

7. When an anthropologist uses the term _____ , he or she is referring to a category of verbal narratives that are secular, non-historical, and seen primarily as a source of entertainment.
   a. folklore
   b. myth
   c. tale
   d. legend
   e. drama

8. Your text describes a type of narrative found in many cultures in which a peasant father and his son, while traveling with their beast of burden, meet a number of people who criticize them.
   What is the motif?
   a. father and son as wise travellers
   b. father as a wise man, son as a young "numbskull"
   c. father as "numbskull," son as a wise individual
   d. father and son trying to please everyone
   e. father and son trying to avoid everyone on their journey

9. The "little songs" of the Bedouin can be best described as _____
   a. anti-structural
   b. forbidden
   c. sung among Europeans only
   d. sung only when the Bedouins are away from their homeland
   e. sung only at marriages

Chapter 13 ➤ *The Arts*

10. The field of ethnomusicology _____ .
    a. is concerned with human music rather than natural music
    b. is the study of music in its cultural setting
    c. began in the nineteenth century with the collection of folk songs
    d. concerns the organization of melody, rhythm, and form in a culture's music
    e. all of the above

11. Who of the following *was not* a member of the Group of Seven?
    a. Emily Carr
    b. F.H. Varley
    c. J.E.H. MacDonald
    d. Franz Johnston
    e. A.Y. Jackson

12. During the Washington Peace March in the sixties, thousands of people sang the song "We Shall Overcome." This song expressed a feeling of common purpose to counteract repression and to reform society. It created a sense of unity among diverse members of the crowd. This example illustrates the _____ of music.
    a. social functions
    b. geographical distribution
    c. tonality
    d. mythological features
    e. polyrhythms

13. Soapstone carvings, a relatively recent innovation, have become a trademark of _____ art.
    a. Bedouin
    b. Inuit
    c. Ju/'hoansi
    d. Nuba
    e. Maori

14. Among the Nuba, colours used for body painting represent different _____ .
    a. age grades
    b. genders
    c. levels of power
    d. age sets
    e. none of the above

15. One of the most intricate forms of tattooing is found among the _____, whose *moko* (facial swirls) are chiselled into the face as a sign of cultural pride.
    a. Aztecs
    b. Incas
    c. Picts
    d. Maori
    e. Gauls

16. Verbal arts include _____ .
    a. narratives
    b. proverbs
    c. dramas
    d. riddles
    e. all of the above

17. The _____ stretched out their ears, inserting increasingly larger plugs and heavier jewellery. This is an example of body adornment.
    a. Kayapo
    b. Mayan
    c. Masai
    d. Inuit
    e. Guyanese

18. In the United States numerous examples exist of marginalized social and ethnic groups attempting to gain a larger audience and more compassion for their plight through song. Perhaps no better example exists than _____.
    a. Mexican Americans
    b. Chinese Americans
    c. Native Americans
    d. Puerto Ricans
    e. African Americans

19. A surprisingly large number of _____ in European and African tales are traceable to ancient sources in India.
    a. stories
    b. myths
    c. motifs
    d. devices
    e. lines

20. The _____ risk their lives to maintain a manly image, engaging in dangerous activities such as deep sea fishing in shark infested waters to prove their manhood.
    a. Inuit
    b. Papua New Guineans
    c. Guyanese
    d. Truk
    e. none of the above

21. The Australian Aborigines have preserved their records of land ownership in song and _____ film.
    a. text
    b. story
    c. clothing
    d. none of the above

Chapter 13 ➤ The Arts

22. Humans are willing to endure pain and discomfort, waste time and resources, and risk chastisement for this type of art.
    a. oil painting
    b. sculpting
    c. pottery
    d. body decoration
    e. cave drawings

23. A true _____ is basically religious, in that it provides a rationale for religious beliefs and practices.
    a. folktale
    b. legend
    c. myth
    d. epic tale
    e. riddle

24. Much of what passes for history consists of the _____ we develop to make ourselves feel better about who we are.
    a. poems
    b. parables
    c. legends
    d. ballads
    e. fictions

25. A surprisingly large number of motifs in European and African tales are traceable to ancient sources in _____ .
    a. China
    b. Japan
    c. Latin America
    d. India
    e. Mesopotamia

26. J.K. Rowling's *Harry Potter and the Philosopher's Stone* (1997) contains many of the best elements of _____ .
    a. legends
    b. folk tales
    c. myths
    d. all of the above
    e. none of the above

27. _____ serve(s)as a powerful way for a social or ethnic group to assert its distinctive identity.
    a. tales
    b. music
    c. chants
    d. poetry
    e. drama

28. Art can affirm group solidarity and identity beyond kinship lines, as evidenced by Canada's

_____ .
    a. turkey
    b. crescent moon
    c. cedar tree
    d. maple leaf
    e. bald eagle

29. In all cultures, the words of songs constitute a kind of _____ .
    a. dance
    b. pain
    c. fear
    d. poetry
    e. joy

30. Tattoos in Western society help satisfy two overarching needs: the need for members to exhibit at least some individuality in an increasingly homogenised world and _____.
    a. the need to be trendy
    b. the need to belong to a group or community
    c. the need for pain
    d. the need to "cool"
    e. none of the above

True/False Practice Questions

1. The term "tale" refers to a type of narrative that is secular, non-historical, and seen primarily as a source of entertainment.
   True or False

2. Legends are semi-historical narratives which recount the deeds of heroes, the movement of peoples, and the establishment of local customs.
   True or False

3. The word "myth," in popular usage, refers to something that is widely believed to be true but probably is not.
   True or False

4. Legends provide clues as to what is considered appropriate behaviour in a culture.
   True or False

5. The use of soapstone in Inuit carvings can be traced back to the Dorset culture (600 BCE–1000 CE).
   True or False

6. Human appearance is a cultural construct as well as a biological given.
   True or False

7. Body art such as tattooing and piercing is generally frivolous and lacks symbolic meaning. True or False

Chapter 13 ➤ _The Arts_

8. The mock wedding is an example of a folk drama.
   True or False

9. During a mock wedding, gender roles are strictly adhered to, with women playing women and men playing men.
   True or False

10. The phenomenon of the "mock wedding" is found throughout Canada.
    True or False

11. In her work *Life Lived Like a Story: Life Stories of Three Yukon Native Elders*, Julie Cruikshank often includes her own analysis and theoretical perspective.
    True or False

12. A true myth is basically religious in that it provides a rationale for religious beliefs and practices.
    True or False

13. For the most part, legends and myths are the products solely of non-literate, non-industrialized societies.
    True or False

14. An art form that has developed recently is tattooing. It involves the puncturing and colouring of human skin with symbolic designs.
    True or False

15. Some form of visual art is a part of every historically known human culture.
    True or False

Short Answer

1. As a type of symbolic expression, visual art may be representational or abstract. Discuss these two categories of visual art.

2. Describe the functional purposes of tattooing.

3. What two dilemmas did Western society face in the 1960s that lead to the increase of tattooing?

4. What is body adornment? Describe the ways in which you adorn your own body.

5. Distinguish between visual and verbal art.

6. Describe the groundbreaking nature of Julie Cruikshank's ethnography *"Life Lived Like a Story: Life Stories of Three Yukon Native Elders."*.

7. What is folklore?

8. Describe the main areas of focus for the ethnomusicologist?

9. Compare and contrast legend and tale.

10. Describe three instances of censorship in the Canadian art world.

Practice Essays

1. Many famous biographies or novels about artists in the West stress the individual creativity of the artist (for example, James Joyce's *Portrait of the Artist as a Young Man)*. Artists are portrayed as people who have the vision to rise above and beyond the social and cultural conditions into which they were born, sometimes even crossing the boundaries of normality as typically defined by society. How is this vision of the artist different from the conception of artists held by non-Western societies?

2. Describe the "Mock Wedding" ceremony of the Prairies. What social function does it perform?

3. Discuss the importance of verbal art for the Australian Aborigines, in terms of their land claim struggles.

4. Describe the cross-cultural similarities surrounding the culture of manhood. What types of images of manliness are evidenced in Canada? Describe.

5. Graffiti has been viewed by government and city officials as vandalism, while certain pieces of graffiti now hang on the walls of Phun Phactory and Halls of Fame in New York. What is your personal stance on graffiti: art or vandalism? Support your claim with evidence from the text.

6. Who were Paul Kane and Emily Carr? Describe their impact on Canadian art.

7. What are the social functions of music? Provide examples.

8. Art in all its forms has countless functions beyond providing aesthetic pleasure. Discuss some of the functions of art.

Chapter 13 ➤ *The Arts*

SOLUTIONS

Fill-in-the-Blank

1. folklore
2. popular
3. Abenaki
4. psuedo-historical
5. India
6. Bedouins
7. ethnomusicolgy
8. songs
9. graffiti
10. polyrhythm
11. stylized
12. Paul Kane
13. entopic phenomena

Multiple-Choice Practice Questions

1. E	11. A	21. C
2. E	12. A	22. D
3. D	13. B	23. C
4. C	14. A	24. C
5. D	15. D	25. D
6. E	16. E	26. B
7. C	17. C	27. B
8. D	18. E	28. D
9. A	19. C	29. D
10. E	20. D	30. B

True/False Practice Questions

1. T	6. T	11. F
2. T	7. F	12. T
3. T	8. T	13. F
4. T	9. F	14. F
5. F	10. F	15. T

CHAPTER 14
THE ANTHROPOLOGY OF HEALTH

SYNOPSIS

Challenge Issues: What is medical anthropology? How do anthropologists approach medical anthropology? How does social inequality affect health and illness? This chapter highlights the ways in which medical anthropology explores how social, cultural, political and historical factors affect health and fitness. The three main approaches to medical anthropology are also considered in this chapter. Finally, the chapter concludes with a discussion of how divisions of class, gender, and ethnicity affect health and considers the role pharmaceutical corporations play in the development of drugs for certain diseases.

CHAPTER OBJECTIVES

- the biocultural approach
- the cultural interpretive approach
- critical medical anthropology
- health and disease in one culture: the Ju/'hoansi
- Vancouver's Downtown Eastside
- women and health
- contemporary biomedicine

KEY TERMS

biocultural approach	environmental justice	medicalization
critical medical anthropology (CMA)	genetic counselling	paleopathology
cultural interpretive approach	guided imagery	
diseases of civilization	medical hegemony	

EXERCISES

Review Questions

1. Define the biomedical approach.

2. Define the cultural interpretive approach.

3. Define critical medical anthropology (CMA).

4. Describe Frank Livingston's research on and interpretation of sickle-cell anemia.

Chapter 14 ➤ *The Anthropology of Health*

165

5. What is the "three bodies" paradigm? Describe each body.

6. What is "mind-body" dualism?

7. Distinguish between disease and illness.

8. What is medical hegemony? How does it relate to the process of medicalization?

9. Who is Margaret Lock? Describe her most recent research.

10. What is shamanism?

11. Describe the use of hallucinogenic drugs among shamans.

12. Where does CMA fit into the broader scope of medical anthropology?

13. How do archaeologists study health from a historical perspective?

14. Describe and distinguish between the general health conditions found among those living in bands and those living in tribal society.

15. What are the five interrelated strands of development associated with the industrial revolution and the modern world system?

16. Who is Dr. Stephen Bezruchka and what are the "Health Olympics"?

17. What factors contribute to poverty?

18. Describe the health risks associated with homelessness.

19. What is environmental justice?

20. What is genetic counselling?

Fill-in-the-Blank

1. CMA stands for _____ _____ _____ .
2. _____ is an approach to medical anthropology that focuses on the study of how cultural beliefs and perceptions of health and illness affect people's health and treatment of disease.
3. The "three bodies" paradigm for use in medical anthropology focuses on the _____ body, the _____ body and the body _____ .
4. According to _____ , when a society feels threatened, it tends to expand the number of social controls through regulation and surveillance.
5. The idea that the "official" theories of health form a kind of orthodoxy, with medical doctors as high priests, is known as _____ .
6. _____ was the dominant form of healing for much of human history.
7. The use of visualization techniques and meditation is known as _____ .
8. The use of direct evidence, such as skeletal remains, as a source of information in the study of health historically and pre-historically is known as _____ .
9. Studies of the forager diet reveal it to be high in _____ and dietary fibre.
10. The wonders of modern medicine and health are _____ distributed around the world.
11. Heart disease, stroke, and cancer are known as _____ _____ _____ .
12. Homeless people throughout North America are experiencing a major resurgence of _____ , a disease that had fallen to low levels after 1945.

Multiple-Choice Practice Questions

1. One early biocultural study, conducted by _____ in 1962, examined adult-onset diabetes among Aboriginal peoples of North America.
    a. Sir Frederick Banting
    b. James V. Neel
    c. Charles Best
    d. John O'Neil
    e. T. Kue Young

2. Two centuries ago, it was the dominant medical belief that a variety of illnesses, from epilepsy to heart disease, could be traced to a single cause: _____ .
    a. possession
    b. poor diet
    c. lack of prayer
    d. excessive smoking
    e. masturbation

3. The paradigm Schepher-Hughes and Lock propose for use in medical anthropology is known as the _____ .
    a. three selves
    b. third body
    c. triple self
    d. triple bodies
    e. three bodies

4. Patriarchy imposes discipline on women's bodies. Which of the following *is not* an extreme example of this imposition?
   a. Chinese foot binding
   b. Victorian corsets
   c. breast-enlargement surgery
   d. tattooing
   e. All of the above are examples of extreme impositions

5. The process by which elements of social and cultural life that had existed outside the realm of medicine are reformulated as medical problems is known as _____.
   a. hegemonizing
   b. medicalization
   c. medicationizing
   d. politicalization of medicine
   e. patriarchy

6. Among the Inuit, shamans are known as _____ .
   a. *curanderos*
   b. angakok
   c. "psychic surgeons"
   d. *nu/um k'xausi*
   e. ebene

7. Shamans often make use of _____ to achieve the trance state.
   a. alcohol
   b. tobacco
   c. dehydration
   d. hallucinogenic drugs
   e. extended periods of activity

8. Cancer patients being talked through a meditation session in which they are asked to imagine, for example, an intense white healing light and visualise it penetrating their bodies, seeking out the site of the tumour and shrinking the tumour, are participating in the practice of
   _____.
   a. guided imagery
   b. medicalization
   c. imaginary healing
   d. health healing
   e. white light imagery

9. The miners described in June Nash's classic study recognized that the _____ system that gave them their livelihood also took their lives.
   a. agriculturalist
   b. horticulturalist
   c. capitalist
   d. disease
   e. industrialized agriculturalist

168   *Chapter 14* ➤ *The Anthropology of Health*

10. The study of ancient skeletal material to reconstruct age at death and cause of death, as well as health, diet, and lifestyle is best described as _____
    a. physical anthropology
    b. biological anthropology
    c. applied anthropology
    d. paleopathology
    e. forensic anthropology

11. The Atkins and Eades diet books mimic a high-protein, low-carbohydrate diet that has existed among most _____ groups.
    a. horticulturalist
    b. agriculturalist
    c. intensive agriculturalist
    d. industrialized
    e. foraging

12. Neolithic populations showed a sharp decline in _____ when compared with their Palaeolithic and Mesolithic ancestors.
    a. fitness
    b. intelligence
    c. hierarchy
    d. work ethic
    e. artistic practices

13. The most striking change brought on by the rise of cities and state societies is _____.
    a. the sharp rise in social inequality
    b. the increase in crowded living spaces
    c. the difficulty in maintaining sanitary conditions
    d. that it brought huge numbers of people together
    e. all of the above

14. The urban revolution produced a permanent division of society into_____ .
    a. commoners
    b. classes
    c. separate but equal groupings
    d. elites
    e. peasants

15. Which of the following was a response to the rise in levels of disease in the early cities and states?
    a. rudimentary public health measures
    b. the emergence of medical specialists
    c. the development of state religion
    d. folk medicine
    e. all of the above

Chapter 14 ➤ *The Anthropology of Health*

16. Evidence suggests that the shift from hunting and gathering to an agricultural subsistence resulted in:
    a. a predictable improvement of overall health status
    b. little change in nutritional status
    c. an overall population decline
    d. an increase in infections and nutritional diseases
    e. none of the above

17. The case of Juan Garcia supports the argument that:
    a. There is an important dynamic to be understood between the individual experience and the global labour processes where patterns of alcohol consumption are concerned.
    b. People make independent decisions with regards to drinking and therefore must face the individual consequences
    c. Tt is possible to conduct significant ethnographic research in Vancouver's Downtown Eastside.
    d. There has been an increase in alcohol consumption of people migrating from Puerto Rico to the United States.
    e. Puerto Ricans are genetically pre-disposed to alcohol addiction.

18. The social safety net can be defined as _____.
    a. a set of governmental agencies and institutions, such as health care
    b. the way in which people socialize
    c. a safe type of interaction
    d. a type of police protection, involving various types of nets
    e. none of the above

19. Ayurvedic medicine comes from which part of the world?
    a. China
    b. India
    c. South Africa
    d. Nepal
    e. The Middle East

20. Which of the following *is not* an example of the so-called diseases of civilization?
    a. heart disease
    b. tuberculosis
    c. stroke
    d. cancer
    e. eating disorders

21. George Manuel and Michael Posluns coined the term _____ to refer to indigenous minorities inside other countries, such as the First Nations peoples in Canada.
    a. disenfranchised
    b. fourth minority
    c. fourth world
    d. northern minority
    e. third world

22. Which of the following statements about the Ju/'hoansi shaman, *n/um k'xau*, is *incorrect*?
    a. They make extensive use of herbal remedies.
    b. The fees they charge are very reasonable.
    c. They work for the good of the community.
    d. They are able to enter trance.
    e. They can magically pull sickness from the body and cast it away.

23. When Botswana achieved independence in 1966, the government made efforts to entice hunter-gatherers like the Ju/'hoansi to settle in one place. Which of the following occurred as a result of the rapid change to Ju/'hoansi culture and lifestyle?
    a. sharp decrease in exercise
    b. loss of a sense of purpose
    c. increased alcohol consumption
    d. increase in blood pressure and evidence of hypertension and heart disease
    e. all of the above

24. In Japan, CEOs make 15 to 20 times what entry-level workers in their factories earn; in the United States, CEOs earn almost _____ times more than entry-level workers.
    a. 100
    b. 200
    c. 300
    d. 400
    e. 500

25. Dara Culhane's work among formerly homeless women in Vancouver's Downtown Eastside illustrates the value of PAR, which stands for _____.
    a. primary action research
    b. participatory area research
    c. primary area research
    d. participatory action rehabilitation
    e. none of the above

26. The over-consumption of this legal product can lead to a wide spectrum of negative consequences, including serious addiction, physical breakdown, domestic violence, and lowered productivity, among other things.
    a. cigarettes
    b. peyote
    c. alcohol
    d. marijuana
    e. none of the above

27. In the 1870s, it was believed that the solution to many female health problems, including tuberculosis, could be cured with the surgical removal of the _____.
    a. ovaries
    b. uterus
    c. breasts
    d. clitoris
    e. fallopian tubes

Chapter 14 ➤ *The Anthropology of Health*

28. In a typical textbook from the 1980s, the terms "degenerate," "decline," "spasms," and "deteriorate" were used to describe this physiological process:
    a. menopause
    b. menstruation
    c. masturbation
    d. mental illness
    e. hysteria

29. Asthma, allergies, skin disorders, and chronic respiratory ailments, as well as birth defects and rare cancers, appeared in disturbingly high numbers in Love Canal, where _____, the most toxic chemical ever created, was dumped by the Hooker Chemical plant.
    a. diotrin
    b. nioxin
    c. niotrix
    d. dioxin
    e. ditrioxicide

30. The main diagnostic test for fetal health, which involves inserting a sterile needle through the abdomen into to uterus in order to withdraw a sample of amniotic fluid, is called_____.
    a. fetal health testing
    b. amniotic testing
    c. amniocentesis
    d. amniobiotechnics
    e. fetal amniotics

True/False Practice Questions

1. Nancy Scheper-Hughes and Margaret Lock developed a paradigm for use in medical anthropology that they call the "three embodiments'
   True or False

2. According to Mary Douglas, when a society feels threatened, it tends to expand the number of social controls through regulation and surveillance.
   True or False

3. The introduction of ritalin, antidepressants and diet drugs exemplify the process of medicaliazation.
   True or False

4. All shamans make use of hallucinogenic drugs to achieve the trance state.
   True or False

5. Many anthropologists support the view that elaborate stage business and bravura performances are key to the shaman's effectiveness as healers.
   True or False

6. For many homeless people, HIV/AIDS is not viewed as a major health risk, even though there is a high rate of prevalence among that subpopulation.
   True or False

7. The Tasmanian Aborigines of Australia are an example of a maladapted people, whose lack of "fitness" caused them to quickly die out.
True or False

8. Due to their strenuous lifestyle, foragers tended to have below-average health.
True or False

9. The shift from foraging to farming lead to an increase in good health and fitness.
True or False

10. Mental illness is culturally contingent.
True or False

11. The pharmaceutical industry is pouring millions of dollars into research on medicines, such as Viagra, which can best be described as a lifestyle drug.
True or False

12. Third world is a term to describe indigenous minorities inside other countries, such as First Nations peoples in Canada.
True or False

13. In parts of Asia and Africa, life expectancy is 37 to 45 years and dropping.
True or False

14. The "Health Olympics" measures international health standards based on athletic testing.
True or False

15. In Japan, there are twice as many men who smoke as compared to America; however, the Japanese have only half as many deaths caused by smoking as Americans.
True or False

Practice Short Answers

1. Describe the changes in health and fitness pre and post independence in 1966 among the Ju/'hoansi.

2. What is participatory action research (PAR)? How does Dana Culhane's research project in Vancouver's Downtown Eastside exemplify this approach?

3. Describe the social conditions that lead to the alcohol-related death of Juan Garcia.

4. Describe the three approaches to medical anthropology and explain how they differ.

5. Define and give two examples of the process of *medicalization*. How would you distinguish it from *medical hegemony*?

6. What is paleopathology and how is it relevant when examining the history of health?

7. Describe the four main responses developed by early state societies to an increase in illness and health hazards.

8. What are the five interrelated strands of development?

Chapter 14 ➤ *The Anthropology of Health*

Practice Essays

1. Where does CMA fit into the broader picture of medical anthropology? What gap in theory and approach does it fill?

2. How does the case study of "Love Canal" contribute to anthropological understandings of health and the environment?

3. How does the placement of the contemporary United States in the "Health Olympics" compare to Japan? Given that both are capitalist nation-states, what accounts for the difference in health status between them?

4. What were the physical and health consequences of the transition from foraging to the Neolithic?

5. What is *genetic counselling*? How does it reflect our changing medical environment?

6. "The personal is political." Discuss this statement with reference to the "three bodies" approach and the work of medical anthropologist Emily Martin.

7. Describe some of the ongoing medical anthropology research in Canada.

8. Which theories of illness, diagnosis, and treatment underline the shamanistic belief systems discussed in the text.

9. Describe the ways in which the medical profession, largely dominated by men, has historically approached the bodies and health problems of women.

10. Describe and discuss the relationship between poverty and health.

SOLUTIONS

Fill-in-the-Blank

1. critical medical anthropology
2. cultural interpretive approach
3. individual, social, politic
4. Mary Douglas
5. medical hegemony
6. shamanism
7. guided imagery
8. paleopathology
9. protein
10. unevenly
11. diseases of civilization
12. tuberculosis

Multiple-Choice Practice Questions

1. B	11. E	21. C
2. E	12. A	22. B
3. E	13. E	23. E
4. D	14. B	24. E
5. B	15. E	25. E
6. B	16. E	26. C
7. D	17. E	27. A
8. A	18. A	28. B
9. C	19. A	29. A
10. D	20. A	30 B

True/False Practice Questions

1. F	6. T	11. T
2. T	7. F	12. F
3. T	8. F	13. T
4. F	9. F	14. F
5. T	10. T	15. T

Chapter 14 ➤ *The Anthropology of Health*

CHAPTER 15
CULTURAL CHANGE
AND THE FUTURE OF HUMANITY

SYNOPSIS

Challenge Issues: How do cultures change? What is modernization? What problems will have to be solved if humanity is to have future? This chapter discusses the mechanisms of cultural change and examines anthropology's role in the changes sweeping the world. The use of the term modernization is considered from a cross-cultural perspective. The chapter concludes with an evaluation of the types of problems, such as the increasing global disparity of wealth and global warming, that will need to be solved in order for humanity to have a future.

CHAPTER OBJECTIVES

- mechanisms of change
- forcible change
- rebellion and revolution
- reproductive rights in Canada
- modernization
- the cultural force of humanity
- aboriginal rights in Canada
- problems of structural violence
- humanity's future

KEY TERMS

acculturation
applied anthropology
cultural pluralism
diffusion
genocide

integrative mechanisms
modernization
primary innovation
replacement reproduction
revolution

secondary innovation
structural differentiation
structural violence

EXERCISES

Review Questions

1. What are four mechanisms of change?

2. Distinguish between primary and secondary innovation.

3. Provide an example of primary innovation.

4. Why is it that cultural context provides the means for innovation to occur?

5. What is diffusion?

6. What is meant by the term "cultural loss"?

7. What is meant by the term "forcible change"?

8. Describe the nature of acculturation.

9. What factors seem to be underlying causes of genocide?

10. What does the field of applied anthropology attempt to accomplish?

11. What is the purpose of revitalization movements?

12. What are the precipitators of rebellion and revolution?

13. What is the problem with the term "modernization"?

14. What are the four sub-processes of modernization?

15. What shortcomings are evident in future-oriented literature?

16. Define and distinguish between structural differentiation and integrative mechanisms.

17. Describe the process of ethnic resurgence.

18. What is cultural pluralism?

19. How does the concept of ethnocentrism interfere with cultural pluralism?

20. Provide examples of structural violence.

21. What is replacement reproduction?

22. Provide some recent examples of environmental pollution.

Fill-in-the-Blank

1. Innovations based on the chance discovery of some new principle are called _____ innovations, while innovations resulting from the deliberate application of these principles are called _____ innovations.
2. The spread of customs or practices from one culture to another is called _____.
3. According to Ralph Linton, as much as _____ percent of a culture's content is due to borrowing.
4. _____ occurs when groups with different cultures come into intensive, firsthand contact and one or both groups experience massive cultural changes.
5. _____is the phenomenon whereby so many carriers of a culture die that those who survive become refugees living among other cultures.
6. The extermination of one people by another is called _____.
7. The field of _____ anthropology uses anthropological knowledge and techniques for practical purposes.
8. The applied work of anthropologist _____contributed to research on Indian Affairs and even the "exotic tribal behaviour of the Ottawa bureaucrat." This anthropologist is also the author of *Making Canadian Indian Policy: The Hidden Agenda 1968-1970* (1981), recognized as one of the twenty best works in English in the Canadian social sciences.
9. The overthrow of a government by force from within is known as _____.
10. Of the roughly 120 armed conflicts in the world today, _____ percent are in the economically poor countries of Africa, Asia and Central and South America.
11. _____ movements are deliberate attempts by members of a society to construct a more satisfactory culture.
12. A revitalization movement that attempts to bring back a destroyed but not forgotten way of life is called a _____, or revivalistic movement.
13. The division of a single traditional role into two or more separate roles, each with a specialized function, is known as _____.
14. Revolutions have occurred only during the last _____ years, since the emergence of centralized systems of political authority.
15. Modernization refers to the process of cultural and socio-economic change whereby developing societies become more similar to _____industrialized societies.
16. The _____ aspect of modernization means a shift in population from rural areas to cities.
17. The Skolt Lapps in the country of _____traditionally supported themselves by fishing and reindeer herding.
18. The Shuar promoted cooperative _____ ranching as their new economic base.
19. Hundreds of millions of people in our world struggle against _____.

178   *Chapter 15* ➤ *Cultural Change and the Future of Humanity*

20. With modernization,_____ find themselves in an increasingly inferior position worldwide.

21. A great deal of the violence in the world is due not to the unique and personal decisions of individuals, but to social, political, and economic conditions; this is referred to as _____ violence.

22. In 1993, the eastern half of the Canadian Northwest Territories became the autonomous territory of _____ .

23. _____ corporations often thwart the wishes of government and systematically overrule foreign-policy decisions.

24. Canada is one of the most culturally_____ countries in the world.

25. The burning of fossil fuels has led to the "greenhouse effect," now more commonly known as

_____.

Multiple-Choice Practice Questions

1. The borrowing of cultural elements from one culture by members of another is known as

_____ .
   a. secondary innovation
   b. modernization
   c. primary innovation
   d. diffusion
   e. acculturation

2. The chance discovery of some new principle that can be applied in a variety of ways is called

_____.
   a. primary innovation
   b. primary syncretism
   c. applied anthropology
   d. millenarism
   e. diffusion

3. The deliberate use of basic ideas in some practical application, such as making use of the knowledge of how electricity works to develop the telephone, is called _____ .
   a. revitalization
   b. millenarism
   c. modernization
   d. integrative mechanism
   e. secondary innovation

4. Copernicus's discovery that the earth orbits the sun rather than vice versa _____ .
   a. was a primary innovation that met the cultural goals and needs of his time
   b. was a primary innovation that was out of step with the needs, values, and goals of the time
   c. was a secondary innovation that put into application the discovery by Ptolemy that heavenly bodies moved on crystalline spheres around the earth
   d. was a secondary innovation that was deliberately developed by Copernicus to destroy the Polish Church
   e. resulted from diffusion of ideas from India

Chapter 15 ➤ _Cultural Change and the Future of Humanity_

5. According to the North American anthropologist Ralph Linton, about 90 percent of any culture's content comes from _____.
   a. primary innovation
   b. diffusion
   c. invention
   d. syncretism
   e. revolution

6. In biblical times, chariots and carts were widespread in the Middle East, but by the sixth century the roads had deteriorated so much that wheeled vehicles were replaced by camels. This illustrates that cultural change is sometimes due to _____ .
   a. primary invention
   b. secondary invention
   c. diffusion
   d. revitalization
   e. cultural loss

7. As a result of prolonged firsthand contact between societies A and B, which of the following might happen?
   a. Society A might wipe out society B, with it becoming a new dominant society.
   b. Society A might retain its distinctive culture but lose its autonomy and come to survive as a subculture such as a caste or ethnic group.
   c. Society A might be wiped out by society B, with only a few scattered refugees living as members of the dominant society.
   d. The cultures of A and B might fuse, becoming a single culture with elements of both.
   e. "Society A might retain its distinctive culture but lose its autonomy and come to survive as a subculture such as a caste or ethnic group," "society A might be wiped out by society B, with only a few scattered refugees living as members of the dominant society," and "the cultures of A and B might fuse, becoming a single culture with elements of both."

8. The extermination of one group of people by another, often deliberately and in the name of progress, is called _____ .
   a. genocide
   b. acculturation
   c. diffusion
   d. applied anthropology
   e. primary innovation

9. The field of applied anthropology developed_____.
   a. through efforts to help the poor in North American society
   b. in sociology classrooms
   c. in industry
   d. in colonial situations
   e. through the efforts of women opposed to prohibition

10. Which of the following was part of the process of acculturation forced upon Aboriginal groups in Canada?
    a.   Children were placed in residential schools in an attempt to Europeanize them.
    b.   Children in residential schools were not allowed to speak their traditional language.
    c.   Children in residential schools were forced to dress like Europeans.
    d.   Children in residential schools had to eat unfamiliar foods.
    e.   all of the above

11. A deliberate attempt by members of society to construct a more satisfying culture may be called
    _____ .
    a.   a secondary innovation
    b.   a revitalization movement
    c.   an enervating movement
    d.   syncretism
    e.   a primary innovation

12. Which of the following is/are considered to be important precipitators of rebellion and revolution?
    a.   There is a sudden reversal of recent economic advances.
    b.   The media no longer support the government.
    c.   The established leadership loses prestige.
    d.   A strong, charismatic leader organizes attacks on the existing government.
    e.   all of above

13. The term "modernization" _____ .
    a.   is a relativistic rather than ethnocentric concept
    b.   refers to the process of cultural and socio-economic change whereby societies acquire the characteristics of industrialized societies
    c.   refers to a global and all-encompassing process whereby modern cities gradually deteriorate
    d.   can be used to show that all societies go through the same stages of evolutionary development, culminating in the urban-industrial state
    e.   is not used by anthropologists

14. As modernization occurs, which of the following changes are likely to follow?
    a.   Literacy increases.
    b.   Religion decreases.
    c.   Kinship plays a less significant role.
    d.   Social mobility increases.
    e.   Literacy increases, religion decreases, kinship plays a less significant role, and social mobility increases.

15. The division of a single role (which serves several functions) into two or more roles (each with a single specialized function) is called _____.
    a.   millenarization
    b.   modernization
    c.   structural differentiation
    d.   industrialization
    e.   diffusion

Chapter 15 ➤ Cultural Change and the Future of Humanity

16. Changes in Skolt Lapp society occurred because _____ .
    a. men switched from reindeer herding to other sources of income
    b. the number of reindeer declined
    c. snowmobiles were used to herd reindeer
    d. society became hierarchical
    e. women became more powerful than men

17. Sally Weaver spent her life promoting justice and recognition for _____ .
    a. the Maori
    b. the Ju/'hoansi
    c. First Nations peoples
    d. the Trobrianders
    e. none of the above

18. The Zapatista uprising in Mexico and the 1950s Algerian struggle for independence from France are both examples of _____ .
    a. adaptation
    b. acculturation
    c. modernization
    d. revolution
    e. urban rebellion

19. Which of the following *is not* defined by theorists as a sub-process of modernization?
    a. technological development
    b. structural diffusion
    c. industrialization
    d. agricultural development
    e. urbanization

20. Drastic cuts to social services, as evidenced in the economic collapse of many East Asian countries in 1997, is an example of what?
    a. structural violence
    b. structural diffusion
    c. urbanization
    d. "one-world" culture
    e. none of the above

21. The eastern half of the Canadian Northwest Territories separated to create the administrative territory of Nunavut in the year   .
    a. 1990
    b. 1991
    c. 1992
    d. 1993
    e. 1994

22. Multinational corporations tend to _____
    a. respond to outside market forces
    b. allow for high levels of transparency
    c. have the ability to overrule foreign-policy decisions
    d. share their information with government and the public
    e. all of the above

23. _____ is violence produced by social, political, and economic structures rather than by the unique and personal decisions of individuals.
    a. torture
    b. modernized violence
    c. structural violence
    d. globalized violence
    e. industrialized violence

24. Pollution, although a worldwide consequence of certain agricultural and industrial activities, is more of a problem in _____ because chemicals that may be banned in richer nations can be used more easily.
    a. poor countries
    b. industrialized countries
    c. arctic countries
    d. Mediterranean countries
    e. ocean areas

25. If a country achieves "replacement reproduction," this means that _____ .
    a. people produce only enough children to replace themselves when they die
    b. each reproductive couple has no more children
    c. its population will immediately stop growing
    d. its population will continue to grow for another fifty years
    e. every other generation can have children

26. The formation of the World Council of Indigenous Peoples in 1975 and the return to an Islamic republic in Iran are examples of _____ .
    a. cultural pluralism
    b. ethnic resurgence
    c. urbanization
    d. modernization
    e. diffusion

27. Ideally, _____ implies a rejection of bigotry, bias, and racism in favour of the cultural traditions of other peoples.
    a. modernization
    b. biocultural pluralism
    c. industrial gentrification
    d. cultural pluralism
    e. cultural gentrification

Chapter 15 ➤ *Cultural Change and the Future of Humanity*

28. In the world society, about three-quarters of the population live in poverty and one-quarter in relative affluence. This can be best be described as _____ .
   a. segregation
   b. global apartheid
   c. pluralism
   d. gentrification
   e. urbanization

29. In order to solve the problems brought about by global structural violence, it has been suggested that dramatic changes in cultural values and motivations, as well as social institutions, will be required. Which of the following would have to change to help solve the problems due to structural violence?
   a. the emphasis on individual self-interest
   b. uncontrolled materialism
   c. a sense of social responsibility
   d. excessive consumption
   e. "the emphasis on individual self-interest," "uncontrolled materialism," and "excessive consumption"

30. The discovery of fired clay by migratory foragers occurred _____ years ago.
   a. 5,000
   b. 15,000
   c. 25,000
   d. 30,000
   e. 45,000

31. The immediate cause of world hunger has less to do with food *production* than with _____ .
   a. food distribution
   b. food destruction
   c. weather patterns
   d. diffusion
   e. acculturation

32. _____ is the massive change that comes about with the sort of intensive, firsthand contact that occurs when dominant societies forcefully expand their activities beyond their borders, leading less powerful societies to abandon their traditional cultures in favour of the foreign.
   a. assimilation
   b. integration
   c. acculturation
   d. adaptation
   e. accommodation

33. In the United States, both government and industry have tried to persuade Aboriginal peoples on reservations experiencing severe economic depression that the solution to their problems would be

    _____.
    a. acculturation
    b. the incorporation of multinational business
    c. communism
    d. to allow the disposal of nuclear and hazardous waster on their lands
    e. none of the above

34. It was not until some time between _____ and _____ years ago that people recognized a highly practical application of fired clay and began using it to make pottery containers and cooking vessels.
    a. 9000 and 8500
    b. 15,000 and 10,000
    c. 30,000 and 25,000
    d. 7500 and 6000
    e. 3000 and 2500

True/False Practice Questions

1. One of the most powerful instruments of diffusion in the contemporary world are the U.S. media.
   True or False

2. Genocide is a recurring problem.
   True or False

3. Brazil's indigenous peoples have shown that they are unable to resist or adapt to demands imposed upon them from outside.
   True or False

4. While the history of assimilating Aboriginal peoples in the United States was more forceful and violent, in Canada assimilation was somewhat more insidious to achieve the same effect.
   True or False

5. Today there is an increasing rate of worldwide poverty.
   True or False

6. The Beothuk currently live in and around Newfoundland.
   True or False

7. Acts of genocide are a fairly recent phenomena.
   True or False

8. Dr. Henry Morgenthaler was a vocal anti-abortionist.
   True or False

9. Revolution, having a history of over 5000 years, is considered to be a relatively ancient phenomenon.
   True or False

10. Because stability is a striking feature of many cultures like the food foragers, subsistence farmers, and pastoralists, these cultures are changeless.
True or False

11. The Shuar case shows that Amazonian nations are unable to control their own destinies.
True or False

12. Multinational corporations are able to ignore and override the wishes of sovereign governments.
True or False

13. Wheeled vehicles virtually disappeared from Morocco to Afghanistan about 1500 years ago. They were replaced by camels because of a reversion to the past by the region's inhabitants.
True or False

14. The practical application of anthropology is thriving today as never before.
True or False

15. In so-called "underdeveloped" countries, women have become a source of cheap labour for large corporations, as subsistence farming has given way to mechanized farming.
True or False

16. The immediate cause of world hunger has more to do with food production than with food distribution.
True or False

Practice Matching

Match the culture with its characteristic.

1. _____ Skolt-Lapps
2. _____ Shuar
3. _____ Eastern Arctic Inuit
4. _____ Beothuk
5. _____ Yanomami

a. a group driven out of their favourite sealing site and shot down like animals by the European settlers in what is now called Newfoundland
b. worked towards splitting Nunavut from the rest of the Canadian Northwest Territories in 1993
c. Indigenous peoples of Ecuador, also known as the Jivaro, who formed a federation to protect their interests
d. Arctic Scandinavians whose society was radically changed by snowmobiles
e. Brazilian group that suffered ethnocide

Short Answer

1. What is applied anthropology?

2. Explain why the Taliban movement in Afghanistan was considered a revitalization movement.

3. Why has it been suggested that, in the near future, it would be impossible for most peoples of the world to achieve something resembling a middle-class standard of living comparable to that of many people in the Western world?

4. What are mechanisms of change?

5. What are the steps involved in modernization?

6. What is the difference between revolution and rebellion?

7. Define culture loss. Provide an example.

8. Why is change essential to cultural survival?

9. Describe the process of leading to extinction with reference to the Yanomami in Brazil.

10. Who was Sally Weaver? Describe her contribution to applied anthropology.

Practice Essays

1. Describe the impact of modernization on Skolt Lapps and Shuar Indians.

2. In what ways can the rising tide of Islamic fundamentalism in the Middle East and other areas of the world be seen as a revitalization movement? Are there other terms from the chapter that could apply to this phenomenon? What might anthropology contribute to our understanding of such movements?

3. Despite a worldwide trend toward "Westernization," and despite the pressure for traditional cultures to disappear, it is clear that cultural differences are still very much with us in the world today. In fact, a tendency for peoples globally to resist modernization, and in some cases retreat from it, is strengthening. Explain ethnic resurgence, using examples.

4. Discuss the rise of multinational corporations and their impact on the domestic as well as the international scene.

5. Explain why revolution is a relatively recent phenomenon.

6. Identify and discuss the problems of structural violence.

7. Reactions of indigenous peoples to changes forced upon them vary considerably. Describe how various groups have reacted to forced change.

8. Belief in "progress"/modernization and its inevitability has important implications for North Americans as well as others. What are some implications? Explain.

Chapter 15 ➤ *Cultural Change and the Future of Humanity*

9. Solving the problems of the global society depends on, among other things, lessening the gap between the living standards of the impoverished and developed countries. How might this be accomplished?

10. "The immediate cause of world hunger has less to do with food *production* than food *distribution*." Discuss.

11. According to Naomi Klein, what process has replaced manufacturing as a primary business strategy of multinational corporations? Explain.

SOLUTIONS

Fill-in-the-Blank

1. primary, secondary
2. diffusion
3. 90
4. Acculturation
5. extinction
6. genocide
7. applied
8. Sally Weaver
9. revolution
10. 98
11. Revitalization
12. revolutionary
13. structural differentiation
14. 5,000
15. Western
16. urbanization
17. Finland
18. cattle
19. poverty
20. women
21. structural
22. Nunavut
23. Multi-national
24. pluralistic
25. global warming

Multiple-Choice Practice Questions

1. D	13. B	25. A
2. A	14. E	26. B
3. E	15. C	27. D
4. B	16. C	28. B
5. B	17. C	29. E
6. E	18. D	30. C
7. E	19. B	31. A
8. A	20. A	32. C
9. D	21. D	33. D
10. E	22. C	34. A
11. B	23. C	
12. E	24. A	

True/False Practice

1. T	7. F	13. T
2. T	8. F	14. T
3. F	9. F	15. T
4. T	10. F	16. F
5. T	11. F	
6. F	12. T	

Practice Matching

1. D
2. C
3. B
4. A
5. E

Chapter 15 ➤ *Cultural Change and the Future of Humanity*   *189*